Being and Listening

Being and Listening

Counselling, Psychoanalysis and the Ontology of Listening

Peter Wilberg

New Yoga Publications

ISBN-13: 978-1483920856
ISBN-10: 1483920852

Content

Content

1. Introduction — 'Being and Listening'

The essential unity or 'belonging together' of *Being and Listening* was nowhere more strikingly affirmed than in a saying of the German thinker Martin Heidegger:

> *"We hear, not the ear."*
> from 'The Principle of Reason' (*Der Satz vom Grund*)

This saying indicates that it is not bodies, bodily sense organs or even the brain that hears but rather *beings* – just as it is also beings that see, speak, sing and make music. To suggest, on the contrary, that it is our ears or brains that hear, is rather like suggesting that just because science could find 'correlations' between the sounds of a Beethoven sonata and the movements of keys on a piano or bow strings on a violin it may be 'scientifically' hypothesised that it is pianos, violins and other musical instruments that create and produce music – and not the *beings* that use them *as* instruments. This of course, is the implicit position of modern brain scientists, obsessed as they are with the 'correlations' that can be found between such activities as hearing, seeing or thinking itself with the activation of different regions of the brain – and who only when pressed will admit that such correlations do not in any way prove that it is brains and not beings that think, see or hear. Heidegger himself was quick to dismiss any such form of reductionism – pointing out that whilst the ear and brain may register the sounds of a Bach fugue, only beings can hear those sounds as *music*, i.e. *as* a Bach fugue. For only a *being* has the capacity to sense and feel *meaning* in whatever they hear.

On the other hand, if there are things *we* are not comfortable hearing – even if only by virtue of being true – we may simply *not* hear them. If this 'not hearing' becomes a habit, it may end up taking the form of an intermittent, progressively worsening or even permanent 'hearing problem'. Indeed, 'hearing difficulties' in general – whether or not they can be medically explained as the result of some physical cause or anomaly in the *ear*, may be a result of being frequently confronted with things *we* don't want to hear – whether as adults, children, or even as babies in the womb (who we know are extremely sensitive to sounds). This would also explain why, just like people *without* a diagnosed 'hearing problem', even those *with* such problems can often be sensed to have inwardly 'cut off' – ceased *listening* – on occasions when something is said to them that they don't want to hear – thus not hearing or hearing with significantly *more* difficulty than at other times.

The German word for hearing is *hören*, which belongs to a family of words including 'to belong' (*gehören*) and 'belonging together' (*Zugehörigkeit*). In this context, Heidegger's essential saying – "*We* hear, not the ear" – also hints at a dimension of mutuality or 'we-ness' in the activity of hearing. And indeed, how a human being addresses us, what they say to us – and the manner in which they say it – is already *a response* to the way in which we are – or are not – listening to them, the silent wavelength or 'tone' of our listening *attunement* to them as beings. Conversely, as Heidegger says: "...if *we* hear, something is not merely added to what the ear picks up; rather, what the ear perceives and how it perceives will already be attuned (*gestimmt*) and determined (*bestimmt*) by what *we* hear..."

Such an ontological 'language of listening', with its roots in a German vocabulary, is one that many have not heard before – and when they do hear it find difficult to follow. It will have an unfamiliar ring to those whose understanding of the counselling relationship is derived from terminologies by Freud or Rogers, or from the 'cognitive' therapies. Hence the aim of this work – to begin to show the as yet un-heard significance of this vocabulary, not just in the narrow context of academic philosophy and Heidegger scholarship, but in a much wider human context. For this is a language which I believe possesses a power to radically deepen our experience of listening, understood not as a mere *prelude* to responding to what someone says, nor as one among other counselling 'skills' or 'techniques' – but rather as something quite different: *as our most primordial mode of being with and 'bearing' with others in pregnant silence*. In particular, it is through being and bearing with others in their suffering, and our own capacity to bear this suffering within us, that the other can come to listen more deeply to themselves, and doing so gestate and give birth to a new 'inner bearing' towards their life world and relationships – a bearing itself based on a deepened capacity for authentic, meditative listening to both themselves *and* others.[1]

"Thinking is a listening which brings into view something one can hear. In so doing it brings into view what was un-heard of."

In the light of this further saying of Heidegger, this work could also have been entitled 'Thinking and Listening'. That is because for over 2,000 years what we call 'thinking' has been identified with verbal reasoning, i.e. with a type of inner *speech* rather than a mode of silent inward listening. That is why revolutions in thought have always gone together with changes in the way people speak about themselves or the world – changes in language. Fundamentalist religions and ideologies each regard the languages, texts as sacred repositories of truth and emphasise the speaking of that Word – even though its origin is often a primordial event of inner *hearing*.

The 'post-modern' intellect sees the essence of truth in the interplay and interweaving of different languages and symbolic systems. Both these viewpoints identify thinking with verbally articulated thoughts. Indeed the Freudian idea of 'unconscious' thought only arises because conscious thought is seen as identical with inner speech – with mental verbalisations. This confuses the verbal products of thinking ('thoughts') with the pre- and post-verbal process of thinking – the inward listening that generates thought.

"Listen not to me but to the *logos*." Heraclitus

Here the Greek word *logos*, as we shall see later, refers not just to a form of speech or verbal account but, more primordially, to the silent inner reverberations of resonances of the soul. Understood in this way, listening is an active attunement to or

---

[1] See also Wilberg, Peter *The Therapist as Listener*, New Gnosis Publications, Chapter 3

resonance with those inner reverberations of the psyche – which both presage and follow the emergence of speech or verbalised thoughts.

The understanding of thinking as a process of listening was thus already anticipated by Heraclitus in the pre-Socratic age of Greek philosophy, just as it was taken up again and refined by Heidegger in the post-Nietzschean age of German philosophy. Between Heraclitus and Heidegger there have been many philosophies of 'reason' and many religions and psychologies of 'the word' but no true philosophy or psychology of listening – a highly symptomatic lack in our society.

What I call 'philosophical counselling' is an embodied philosophical psychology of listening. It unites Heidegger's philosophical understanding of listening with the psychological understanding of thinking developed by the 'independent' school of psychoanalysts in Britain. It was Winnicott who first linked the development of 'thinking' with the infant's capacity to wait for the mother. The infant-mother relation finds its parallel in the adult's relation to the 'mother tongue.' In listening we wait in silence for the mother tongue to provide us with verbalised thoughts. Freud saw silence as a characteristic expression of 'resistance' to the verbalisation of unconscious thoughts. Heidegger, on the other hand, saw society's resistance to silence as a flight from meditative thinking. It is silence that allows thinking and speech their gestation phase. What we call 'character' is an individual's capacity to be in silence, and thus to bear the generative process of thinking – a process of inward listening.

Conventional communication patterns, however, work to close uncomfortable gaps of silence, prematurely filling them with spoken or mental words. This forecloses our capacity for inward listening, and replaces the process of thinking with the acquired thoughts and preconceptions embodied in our habitual language and vocabulary.

Marx wrote "The philosophers have only interpreted the world. The point, however, is to change it." Philosophies can only change the world if they express and stimulate new ways of listening. Conversely, profound insights only arise through finding deeper ways of listening to ourselves and to others. This applies not only to individuals, but to groups and whole nations.

There are many mute voices that remain unheard in the individual and in society because we lack ways of listening that allow us to acknowledge and respond to them. This can present serious dangers for society, as it did in Heidegger's Germany – resulting in 'evils' that are always easier to label in words than the lack which spawns them.

In his 'Introduction to Metaphysics' (1935) Heidegger wrote: "Philosophy is essentially untimely because it is one of those few things that can never find an immediate echo in the present. When such an echo seems to occur, when a philosophy becomes fashionable, either it is no real philosophy or it has been misinterpreted and misused for ephemeral and extraneous purposes."

In adapting itself to contemporary fashions and fads, thinking ceases to deepen our under-standing. For then it no longer stands *under* such trends – is no longer subversive. We might also add 'philosophy' is always conservative. To conserve the heritage of a great thinker such as Heidegger does not mean to turn his work into the object of academic scholarship. Paradoxically, the more people write *about* what Heidegger said and thought, the less they attempt to embody what he did – the praxis that his thinking embodied, and in particular, his way of listening. As a result his thinking is not conserved but emasculated. Philosophical counselling is an attempt to conserve a way of thinking and listening that can be experienced, explored and embodied but never institutionalised. This attempt is extremely untimely given the domination of institutional training in counselling by a language which reduces it to a diverse and more or less eclectic set of frameworks, skills, methods and techniques.

As John Heaton pointed out, in Greek and Roman time philosophers treated disorders of the soul "which in modern times have been medicalised under the name of neurosis." This is because, for the ancients, philosophies were ways of living and ways of being. "Thus the Greeks and Romans were very interested in how the philosopher lived his life and how he died. For the mark of the philosopher was that he was not a slave to pleasure and pain and he had overcome irrational fears of death."

Heraclitus was not a 'certified', 'accredited' philosopher equipped with a pre-determined set of skills. Nor was Freud an accredited, trained, supervised or even analysed analyst when he began to develop psychoanalysis. Today counsellors are trained and analysts must be analysed. Yet there is truth in Heaton's statement that: "The great advance Freud made was to make psychotherapy a technique so that anyone could become a therapist provided he knew how to apply the technique; the possession of a valid certificate given by an institution becomes the criterion rather than a judgement of a way of life."

There are good grounds for disagreeing with the idea that psychoanalysis is reducible to a technique. How else, however, can it be a 'provable' or 'proven' therapy in medical terms? And if it is not a technique the question is, what is it?

This question is not a scientific one but a philosophical one. So are the questions put by Steven Gans:
"Who is an analyst? What is the difference between the analyst and non-analyst?
Between analysis and non-analysis? Is there psychoanalysis?
What is an appropriate way to speak of work inside analysis, of the project of *listening to another and to other than consciousness?* "

It was the Swiss psychiatrist Medard Boss who wrote of the contribution that 'existential analysis' – Heidegger's *Daseinsanalytik* – could render to psychoanalysis. The quotations above are taken from the first issue (1990) of the journal of the Society for Existential Analysis – founded to "provide a forum for the analysis of existence" from philosophical as well as psychological perspectives. 1988 saw the publication of 'Existential Counselling in Practice' by Emmy van Deurzen-Smith. In this work she questions the sufficiency of 'listening and empathic responding' in counselling.

"Only in so far as the existential counsellor is firmly at one with herself will she be capable of hearing the meaning of the client's words, spoken or unspoken. It is *not merely a matter of being there for the client and listening.*"

The difference between 'existential counselling' and what I call 'philosophical counselling' is to do with the word 'merely.' The purpose of this work is to question more deeply what 'being there for the client and listening' means. It advances a philosophical psychology of listening that is relevant to counselling precisely because it transcends ordinary counselling concepts of 'empathic responding'. The value and importance of listening in individual and social life itself transcends the entire sphere of counselling as a social and institutional role. Philosophical counselling belongs to what I call 'Third Ear Education' – a project to take the art of listening beyond the social and institutional confines of the 'counselling' role and to restore an understanding of 'philosophy' as a way of *listening and being.*

2. Philosophy and Counselling – basic questions

This book raises six key questions concerning the relation between counselling and philosophy. In discussing these questions I introduce the notion of a 'philosophical counselling' – one rooted in a philosophical understanding of listening, being and thinking. The questions are:

- What is the relation between philosophy and counselling?
- What is the basis of current counselling philosophy?
- What sort of questions should a philosophy of counselling address?
- What does it mean to counsel philosophically?
- What is the basic stance and tone of the philosophical counsellor?
- What type of education and awareness can awaken a philosophical stance in counselling?

In addressing these questions I draw not only on the thinking of Heidegger and Winnicott, but also on the ethical philosophy of the German-Jewish thinker Martin Buber. The relevance of these thinkers to the questions formulated above cannot be overestimated, even though they figure only marginally in the theoretical literature on counselling and psychotherapy. The questions formulated above have also been marginalised, taking second place to an emphasis in all institutionalised forms of counselling theory on 'theory', 'techniques', 'skills', 'training' and 'supervision'.

Institutionalised approaches to counselling have one common denominator – they imply that it makes no essential difference to a client who their professional listener is – as long as they are 'professional' and listen in the 'right' way. It is this fundamental separation of *listening* and *being* which this essay seeks to question. An adequate philosophy of counselling, I argue, requires a depth psychology and philosophy of listening – something that is sorely lacking in the entire literature on counselling, psychotherapy and psychoanalysis. Such a philosophy cannot separate listening and being, for to listen with our whole being is also to communicate our whole being – and must be, if we are to *tune* our being to another individual. In doing so we also convey the essential *tone* of our own being – which becomes a carrier wave on which messages are not only received but also transmitted wordlessly by the listener.

How we perceive someone when we do so communicates directly and wordlessly, modulating the tone of our listening and sending messages that ride on this tone. To see listening merely as a prelude to verbal response, is to mis-understand its nature as a form of wordless inner response – one that communicates directly from our being. Irrespective of any processes of 'transference' or 'counter-transference' people mean something to one another because of who they are. Being communicates. To understand a client's words means to 'under-stand' them – take a stand *under* language and in being. This means relating from our being rather than through outward postures or posturing.

The word client derives from the Latin *cluere*. It means 'to be called'. To 'empathise' with a client is also to *be* a 'client' – to be silently recalled to one's own being through the words of another. It also means to silently respond to this call *from* one's being as well as in words. A philosophical approach to counselling is therefore not something abstract or 'theoretical'. Nor can it be reduced to a set of skills or a formalised training procedure. Its focus is the characteristic *inner bearing* of both counsellor and client – the way they bear themselves in silence and allow themselves to be 'called' within it. In other words, the way they listen or do not listen – their capacity for *hearkening* to and *heeding* this call. 'Hearkening' and 'heeding' are two 'keywords' I introduce for a new way of listening, one distinct from current counselling practice.

It was Heidegger who first recalled this language of listening. My main explicit source, however, will be the sayings of the Greek thinker Heraclitus (500 BC) – the first *psychologist of listening*. Heraclitus lived during an era of growing scepticism towards the multiple gods of Homeric mythology, affirming for the first time the essentially philosophical nature of the human quest for meaning.

Our 'post-modern' era is also one in which the ideological gods of recent centuries, including Freud – are losing their aura prestige. They have given way to different gods – the Market, Competition, Technology and Genetics. The difference today is that both old and new gods have become hidden gods, not worshipped openly in temples but covertly in speech – as verbal icons. The different schools of counselling, analysis and therapy house and guard their gods in different temples of language, competing professional terminologies. The post-modern attitude celebrates this polytheistic diversity, yet all the different ways of speaking about the psyche cause confusion in the mind of the layman, arouse suspicion from the general public and indirectly promote counter-movements of conservatism and fundamentalism that restore old and hallowed names for the One. And yet "The wise is one alone, willing and unwilling to be spoken of by the name of Zeus." For Heraclitus, acknowledging the one-ness of being was not the same things as naming this One in words. Loving this One – the *sophon* – meant listening to the inner speech or *logos* of the *psyche* – its wordless resonances.

Neither a plurality of different ways of naming what is important and meaningful to us in words, nor the privileging of a single Name or interpretative language suffice. Different ways of speaking about ourselves and others do not substitute for a deepening of the way we listen. This requires that we listen also to our own personal and professional language – recognising its implicit and often conflicting gods. For a counsellor this is especially important, for whatever their training and however deep their experience, both are couched in a particular language. But the aim of counselling is to help others to take a stand under their own language and its icons – the habitual vocabulary with which they think and talk about themselves.

Wittgenstein: 'The limits of my language are the limits of my world." Put in an affirmative way – the way we *word* ourselves is the way we *world* ourselves. Wording is worlding.

Heraclitus was a *logosopher* rather than a philosopher in the modern or post-modern sense. His was a wisdom of the *logos*. Philosophical counselling is not psychoanalysis or philosophy but a 'logotherapy' in this original sense. For Viktor Frankl, 'logotherapy' meant a form of therapeutic counselling based on what he called 'the will to meaning'. I relate the personal and inter-personal questions addressed by counselling to the 'philosophical' quest for meaning and to the fundamental questions of philosophy – questions of being. Personal and inter-personal problems always go together with a more or less painful sense of separation from our own 'pre-personal' or 'trans-personal' being. This sense of not being fully ourselves nags at us like an unstated question. Not so much a question as a 'quest-ion'- a wordless questing of our being for wholeness.

3. Philosophical and Counselling Dialogue – 'questioning' and 'questing'

Philosophy, as we know it from Plato's Socrates is a dialogue and a process of questioning. So is counselling. In both forms of dialogue questions are stated and explored without being finally answered. Both the philosopher and the counsellor also listen for questions that are unstated and merely implied. Many of the unstated and unexplored questions raised in philosophical dialogues are personal ones. They are not propositions to be argued but concern the philosopher's personal inner relationship to what is being talked about. Conversely, many of the unstated and implicit questions raised in counselling dialogue are philosophical ones – they brook no easy answer because they are not problems to be solved but questions to be experienced – questions that we all live. The historical relation between philosophy and counselling is the relation between philosophy and life – it has to do essentially with the relation between stated and unstated questions, questions that are asked in words and questions that are personally lived, that are posed and answered by life.

The questions we confront in our lives are more than just personal or psychological questions. Instead they are always rooted in shared 'philosophical' questions of existence – 'pre-personal', 'inter-personal' or 'trans-personal'- that address both counsellor and client. No counsellor or therapist can answer a client's questions. Nor can counsellors dissociate themselves from these questions as if they were the private property of the client. Clients often come to counselling not just because they face difficult questions, nor even because they feel alone in dealing with these questions, but because they feel it is their question alone. The underlying question they address to the counsellor is "Am I the only person experiencing this problem?" The answer is always yes and no. Yes, because we each confront and respond to fundamental life questions in a different way. No, because underneath all issues relating to our personal psychological responses to life's challenges remain questions which we all share – questions which are 'philosophical' not because they are abstract but because they are living questions – part of the very fabric of life. If this is not fully recognised, our compassion for a person's problems and suffering, their very skill in helping them to see new emotional or practical aspects of the questions they face, can implicitly add to the client's sense of being the question's sole bearer.

Most people come to counselling not out of full awareness of questions facing them but out of an awareness that, whatever problem it is that confronts them, there is some question lurking within it that they have not yet found or asked themselves. That is to say, they are not groping for an answer so much as groping for the question. The counsellor may be aware that questions a client raises with regards to the precipitating or 'presenting' problem only skim the surface, and yet the client may cling to these questions for fear of being totally in the dark without them.

A question we are in the dark about is a situation or condition (social, physical or psychological) that lingers and 'nags us' despite all our attempts to reduce it to a superficial practical question or to respond to it – answer it – in our habitual ways. Nagged or oppressed in this way we feel not quite ourselves, apart from ourselves, and not fully whole in our being. The 'real question' as opposed to the 'surface' question – the philosophical question – is not essentially thematic. It does not have to do with our infantile or childhood past or even our existential future. It is not a question 'about' anything practical, nor is it a question 'about' an existential theme such as death, freedom, meaning, values, etc. The philosophical question is the question that we experience wordlessly – it is the very apartness from ourselves that nags or oppresses us through the presenting problem. It is a question not of what we experience but of how and whom we experience ourselves to be – a question of being. Not a question we 'have' but a question that 'has us' – that expresses a rift in our very being.

The verbal questions that we pose to ourselves are false not because they are irrelevant or unimportant. They may be extremely important. They are false in so far as they can only be answered by first surrendering to the underlying question – the sense of apartness from ourselves and the negative relation to ourselves that goes along with this – our dislike for the situation we are in, what we are feeling, what we have done or have to do, etc. Surrendering to the inner question as a question of being means acknowledging the reality of the situation – not what it is but that it is. It also means acknowledging that we do not merely 'have' a problem but that in essence we are the problem. The apartness we feel from ourselves as a result of the problem, and our inability to fully be ourselves in the face of this problem, is the problem.

To allow ourselves to be the question, to acknowledge this apartness from ourselves, is painful. Or rather what we call 'pain' is this very sense of apartness from our own being, whether experienced through a physical or psychological condition. A question is painful because it demands an unconditional surrender of all our previous question and answers. To abandon our superficial questions however, is not the same as abandoning all hope of an answer. Quite the contrary, for by 'being the question' we turn our mental and verbal questioning into an authentic questing of our being. In turn, we open ourselves to receiving an answer from our own being.

The moment we allow ourselves to be the question we begin to become the answer – for we begin to acknowledge all those aspects of ourselves that we have hitherto kept at a distance by objectifying them in the form of an outer or inner 'problem'. The moment the question becomes fully and wholly a question of being is the moment we begin again to become whole as beings – to heal. This healing or becoming whole, no longer feeling apart from ourselves, is the fundamental change that allows us to receive new answers to our surface questions – answers that are authentic because they arise from a transformation of our being. Or to put this in slightly different terms – by questing with our being we open ourselves to receiving an answering call from our being, whether in the form of an insight, a chance event or opportunity, an expansion of perspective or a spontaneous sense of relief, a lightening of our burden.

The burden of a problem is like the burden of a pregnancy. We carry or bear the question that we have not yet answered as a burden that we cannot alleviate by merely talking about it. Physical symptoms, no less than psychological distress, are both a form of pregnancy. What is pregnant in both is a transformation of our self-being. This need for transformation may be experienced as distress (in fact the German word for 'need' is the same as that for 'distress' – *Not*). What precipitated or seeded the pregnancy is one thing. Attempts to accelerate or abort it are another. 'Being the question' means acknowledging the need – the child – as our own. Listening is its gestation – allowing us to 'become the answer'.

> *"A disposition can confine man in his corporeality as in a prison. Yet it can also carry him through corporeality as one of the paths leading out of it. "* Heidegger

4. Presuppositions of Counselling — identity as private property

All experience is both experience of something other than self (a thing, person, situation or event) and self-experience (something that colours our experience of ourselves). What we experience, inwardly or outwardly, always impinges to some extent on our self-experience – on who we experience ourselves to be. Yet the linguistic ego – the word 'I' – constantly reinforces the notion of a self that stands over and above its own experiences. The very structure of language implies a Subject separate and immune from its own Verbs and Objects – as if my self-experience when 'I' listen to profound music were the same as when 'I' fill in a tax return form. By separating self-experience into two parts, an unchanging 'I' and the (changing) experiences that it 'has', language transforms our self-being into personal identity bounded by the linguistic ego. Conversely, it is through this ego that we guard these identity boundaries, preventing what we do and feel from affecting and altering our self-experience. By splitting self-experience into self + experience, language also separates self-experience from our experience of others and otherness. In this way it transforms experience and identity into the private experiential property of persons – 'I' and 'you', 'him' and 'her', 'us' and 'them'. This creates a rift between language and being, one that makes rifts in our own self-being appear as rifts between persons, between self and other. It is this rift between language and being that makes us see our problems as 'personal' ones only rather than as questions of being.

The value of philosophy for counselling is to introduce a language of being that overcomes the notion of identity as private property. Nowhere in the current language of counselling, however, do we find a language of being. Instead we find a language of personal and inter-personal boundaries. The philosophical assumption here is that boundaries are what separates people, families and nations – that two individuals, like two countries, can either maintain their boundaries as separate personal identities or dissolve these boundaries – fuse to become one. This assumption goes together with the belief that the function of the counsellor's role 'boundaries' is to separate their own experience from that of the client, to 'own' their identity as private property and help clients to do the same. In responding to the questions facing their clients counsellors will of course draw on their own life experience. Indeed they will tend to attract clients for whom this experience is particularly valuable. By sharing their experience in this way, even if only indirectly, they acknowledge a level at which all experience is experience of something shared and all questions are shared questions. As we have seen however, even compassion and insight can be isolating to the client, if the basic inner stance of the counsellor is not a philosophical one in this sense – does not acknowledge essential questions and dimensions of experience as shared ones. Psychology then becomes a substitute for the philosophical recognition that on a deeper level all questions are shared and none are finally 'resolved'. These philosophical questions have to do with the questing of our being for meaning and wholeness and it belongs to the essence of living to keep basic questions alive in our soul as a questing – as 'quest-ions'.

Solving existential or emotional problems is not the same thing as answering fundamental questions – questions of being. Psychological problems are questions that are experienced as personally painful because they bring to light a rift within our own being. And yet the questing of our being for wholeness is never finally resolved. This is why, although insight into different psychological or practical aspects of a question helps people to solve their problems (and in this way to make their experience of these questions less 'painful') it does not answer those questions as questions of being – as 'quest-ions'.

Questions may become more painful than necessary by seeing them merely as problems to be solved – the temptation of the client, or believing that in answering questions one has resolved the quest that underlies them – the temptation of the counsellor.

To do so is to foreclose the quest-ion, thereby adopting a stance that is implicitly inferior (I haven't resolved this quest-ion but others seem to have) or superior (I have solved some problems relating to this quest-ion therefore I have resolved it).

There is a difference, then, between solving problems and believing that in solving these problems one has resolved the underlying quest-ions. This difference comes to life when a client's problems raise issues that seem 'coincidentally' to be very 'close to home' – that mirror current and unresolved problems in the counsellor's own life. It is then that the latter may feel inadequate or destabilised in their role boundaries, afraid of 'counter-transference' or of 'projecting' their own feelings onto the client. This is one expression of a basic paradox. For the more we seek to separate our own experience from that of others the more insecure our boundaries become.

Shared quest-ions are like shared boundaries – on one side is my response to the quest, on another side is yours. These responses are what distinguishes us as human beings. Yet they are also what draws us together in a common quest. It is by staying with the question as a common quest-ion that we both acknowledge the shared dimension of all questions – their reality as 'questions of being'- and at the same time distinguish ourselves as beings. The questions posed by a counsellor do not simply mirror the questing of the client or meet their request for support and assistance. They also express the questing of the counsellor, a search to discover new aspects and dimensions of shared quest-ions.

Letting go of surface questions may seem to both counsellor and client like a form of resignation. When we become aware of a gap between language and being we either become speechless or escape into verbal curiosity – what Heidegger called 'idle talk'. Wordlessness is a withdrawal from idle talk and superficial language. It is often seen and experienced as a symptom of depression. The retreat from superficial language and questions may seem like an act of resignation – giving up our life-quest and our quest for life. And yet it is this very retreat that allows us once again to wordlessly experience the questing of our being for wholeness and meaning, and with patience to find words for our own quest-ions – not dead words but living words. In philosophy and in counselling one question leads to another. The question is whether they lead us away from or towards our own being.

Questing is what we do when we allow ourselves to be the question. In music, a single note or chord might tremble with a certain incompleteness and in this sense quest a response from an answering chord or note. There are no verbal questions and answers in a piece of music, and yet we hear in its tones a constant questing and response. The same is true of the music of feeling. It is through tones of feeling that we quest an answering response, not in words but from answering tones that communicate *dia-logos*: not in but through the word.

5. Towards a Philosophy of Listening — 'empathy' and 'attunement'

Like questions, feelings too are not essentially the *private property* of persons. They are tones of being – shared wavelengths of attunement that connect us to our own being and at the same time link and join one being with another. They are 'boundaries' that join. If a counsellor tells a client that 'I detect some fear in you' this implies that the counsellor either identifies a signal of the client as an indication of fear, or that she herself 'senses' this fear – feels it to some extent herself. But even to identify a signal as a signal *of* something implies a capacity to identify with what is behind that signal – to feel it. In both cases therefore, 'empathy' is involved – emotional identification. And yet the language of the statement 'I detect some fear in you' is a language of emotional *dis-identification*. 'I' only 'detect' this 'fear', which is essentially 'in you'. The counsellor regards herself as having spontaneously 'tuned into' the client's fear rather than as having intentionally tuned herself to the client on a wavelength of feeling that she herself chooses to represent by the word 'fear'.

It is by translating our feelings into nameable emotions belonging to persons that they become private emotional property – 'mine' or 'yours', 'his' or 'hers'. The structures of language constantly translate what goes on between human beings into something going on 'in' persons – 'in' me or 'in' you, 'in' him or 'in' her. In describing our feelings in these terms we fail to question and understand the language of emotional discourse philosophically – to take a stand under and beneath this language and its structures. To do so means focussing not on what is going on 'in' people so much as what is going on in what Martin Buber called the 'between', the space of our relationality.

Relationality is determined by our attunement to another being. The German word for 'determine' is *bestimmen*, related to *Stimme* (voice) and *Stimmung* (tone or mood). The formal meaning of *bestimmen* is to determine or to destine – to hold sway over. It's essential meaning is something like 'to set a tone'. The way we attune to another person sets a tone, determines or holds sway over how we perceive them. This does not mean that our perceptions are mere 'projections'. For if they were we would not be 'tuned in' at all. It is precisely because we are tuned in and not merely projecting that we also determine the wavelength of that attunement – as we do on a radio receiver. Feeling tones are the carrier waves on which a listener not only receives but also transmits messages to a speaker – wordlessly relaying their *listening response*. Someone may tune into a radio music station and describe the music that they hear as 'fearful'. Another person may describe it quite differently. Both descriptions are translations of something essentially wordless – music – and something that we hear only because we have tuned into it, set a certain 'frequency' or 'wavelength' of attunement. Musical tones only speak to us if we really attune to them with our feelings – if we let them echo our feeling tones. We only really listen to music when we listen through the music to ourselves – for it is by attuning to it with feeling that it recalls us to our being.

The feeling tones with which we attune to someone not only allow us to hear the music of their feelings – they recall us to our own being and echo its 'toning'. How a counsellor hears and responds to another person's feelings therefore always has to do with the music they are playing – the tone and tune of their listening attunement (*Bestimmung*). It also has to do with their own language – how they interpret these tones in the vocabulary of the emotions, and what or who they attribute these emotions to.

The term 'emotional empathy' is itself a substitute for a philosophy of listening and feeling that explores the inner nature of 'attunement' and 'rapport'. Given the proliferation of theories and schools of counselling it is surprising that there has not yet been any attempt to formulate a depth philosophy or psychology of listening. And despite its obvious centrality to psychotherapy and psychoanalysis the very word 'listening' is hardly to be found in the entire therapeutic and analytic literature. In psychoanalysis a philosophy and psychology of listening is replaced by theoretical 'listening perspectives' – conceptual frameworks of understanding and interpretation. In counselling literature it is replaced by listening 'skills' and 'techniques'. These deal only with how a counsellor should or should not respond outwardly to a client – how to give the 'correct' outward appearance of listening through body language, verbal responses, etc. They do not quest the real meaning of listening – what it is.

6. The First 'Psychologist' of Listening — Heraclitus

It is the greatest arrogance to think that it is only through modern psychological theories and 'sciences' that we can truly understand the nature of the psyche, or of mental or 'psychological' distress or 'illness'. This is not least because it was the ancient Greek thinker Heraclitus who was the first 'psychologist' – for it is in a saying of his that the Greek words *psyche* and *logos* are conjoined and collocated for the very first time in history. The saying reads: "You will not find out the limits of the *psyche* by going around it, so deep is its *logos*." For Heraclitus then, *logos* meant something like the inner resonance or reverberation of the psyche, a reverberation or 'report' so deep we can never trace it by 'going around it' – by circumscribing it in language. This resonance precedes speech and outer hearing; which is why he could say "men fail to comprehend it, both before hearing and once they have heard", and, even more importantly for our purposes: *"Not knowing how to listen, neither can they speak."* The Stoic philosophers who followed him distinguished between verbal utterance (*logos prophorikos*) and the silent or 'inner' word of the psyche (*logos endiathetos*). Language is something we share in common. Yet it was not language – the *logos prophorikos* – that Heraclitus was referring to when he said "Although this logos is shared, most men live as though their sensibility were a private possession."

The way we translate this *logos* into words shapes the way we fulfil and realise our being in worldly terms. Wording is 'worlding' – the way we shape our own experience in word and deed, and through it create our personal reality. A language governed by verbal polarities of whatever sort – 'success' vs 'failure', 'joy' vs 'pain', 'high' vs 'low', 'intellect' vs 'emotion', 'transference' vs 'counter-transference', 'counselling' vs 'philosophy', 'speaking' vs 'listening' – creates a life-world governed by these polarities. Only our listening can transcend these verbal polarities. Thought itself is an oscillation between this outer and inner logos, between words and the wordless resonances of the psyche. This oscillation has its own inner sound and its own meaning – its own tone and intentionality. The problem today is that we identify thinking only with verbally articulated thoughts, and that the logos of Heraclitus has been reduced to the scientific '-ologies' – biology, sociology, psychology, etc. or else formalised as a calculative 'logic' or 'logistics' – serving the company 'logo'.

Listening to the *logos* has been reduced to listening to the 'logical' structures or contradictions of propositions and statements – not to the unstated or implicit word. As a result, the wordless dimension of thinking has been lost not only to science but to philosophy. Psychoanalysis acknowledges this dimension of thinking through the concept of the 'unconscious' but does so using 'psychological' terminologies that are themselves based primarily on verbal reasoning, interpretation and 'logic'. As a result there is a confusion of competing theories and terminologies, none of which reclaim their linguistic roots and the *etymos logos* – the truth of the word. By listening to language philosophically we can re-link meanings that words have divided and polarised.

Heidegger heard in the Greek word *logos* an echo of the related Greek verb *legein* – to gather. This echo can still be heard in the English expression 'I gather'. Listening is *legein* – a gathering of impressions. 'Listen to the logos' means attending to what is gathering within us – letting it ripen and mature before seeking to harvest it in words or mental pictures. Even to describe what gathers in terms of nameable emotions or thoughts, or to challenge it forth with questions, however 'open', can give premature birth to the *logos prophorikos* and foreclose our listening. And yet this is exactly what much counselling practice encourages by its emphasis on verbal echoing, mirroring, summarising and questioning. Most training in so-called listening skills is based on a negative definition of listening – not interrupting, not giving advice, not answering questions for the client, etc. There is no positive understanding of what listening itself really is – of the wordless activity of attuning and gathering.

Philosophy in Heraclitus's sense did not mean 'talking philosophy' but listening philosophically. Philosophy and counselling are both rooted in listening – meditative listening. Neither involves simply asking or answering questions. Both involve hearing and responding to the unstated and shared questions implied by people's words. Hearkening to the wordless questing of each other's being. Meditative listening is not questioning but questing. It is the way we attend questingly to language, to being, and to speaking beings – human beings. "Man's character is his fate". The Greek word for fate is *daimon* - an inner being. Character is our relation to this being – whose silent voice is a questing and destining voice, one that leads us upon our own way of being.

7. Following and Leading — a way and ways

As well as *gathering*, listening also implies following and leading people along their own way of being. To follow someone means being able to stay with them on this way. Our 'post-modern' world, however, is one in which countless ways of being, ways of thinking and ways of living exist side by side and in competition with one another. This makes following difficult, for each person searches for a way of following their own values and interests, within the maze of competing ways. Some attempt to do this by individualistically refusing to follow others along their way. Others seek sanctuary in the words or beliefs of others, forming communities of 'followers'. Yet following is not a sanctuary in which we stay put. Following means following a way — wherever it might lead us.

One purpose of counselling is to help others to follow their own values, feelings and impulses along whatever way they might lead. We use words to construct signposts along the way. These can also lead us astray. To follow a way is not simply to follow the signposting of language but to explore paths and destinations that are off the track and not yet named by these signposts. To help another person to follow their way means helping them to understand how their existing signposts can literally mis-lead. The crossroads we come to at different stages of our life is also marked by our old signposts. To make important life decisions means first questioning the words and verbal signposts by which we define our alternatives. Change always involves choice or re-choice. But real change is always marked also by a change in the way that we define those choices, by changes in our verbal signposting that are reflected in our language itself.

To follow a different way means to erect new and different signposts for ourselves – instead of clinging to our old language and its signposts whenever we lose our way or come to a crossroads. It means following and speaking a new language. Losing our way – no longer having clear verbal signposts to follow – can be the first step. Taking time to listen to ourselves means taking time to stop at any cross-road and question the value and meaningfulness of the signposts that mark it. Listening – following another person as they speak – we get a picture of the mental railtracks and highways marked by their existing vocabulary and the emotional traffic that moves along them. But a listening that helps another to follow their way rather than rush along inherited and pre-established roadways and tracks is a listening that also leads people gently off these tracks and roadways. No listening that merely follows someone's speech – however 'empathically', can help a person to be led by their own being. To be led by our being means to be led by a listening that hearkens to being, rather than blindly following the ways of language. To help another person to be led on their own way of being means helping them to be led by a listening that hearkens to their own being rather than to their existing language. A listening that helps another person to hear and follow themselves is a listening that leads as well as follows.

"From tones at variance comes perfect attunement." A listening that leads is not one that merely attunes empathically to the tones of the speaker's voice, words and feelings but one that also sets a tone at variance with these. This variant tone is not a counter-tone struck by the listener's verbal responses and interpretations but a silent and wordless tone – the fundamental tone of the listener's own being. To follow someone means to be there 'with' them and to stay with them. But we cannot be with someone fully unless we are fully there to ourselves – unless we stay with our own being and its fundamental tone. That is why listening can never be reduced to a set of skills and techniques that we learn in order to listen 'in role' – to listen as a counsellor, as a teacher, as a manager, etc. Training in listening 'skills' and 'techniques' implies that it makes no difference who is listening as long as the listening is done in the 'right' way – conforming to the specifications of the role. It presupposes that whilst it makes a difference to a client how 'good' a counsellor is in applying these skills and techniques it makes no essential difference to the client who the counsellor is, as long as what they do and how they do it is reasonably 'good'. As a result, the trainee counsellor is not truly called upon to listen to and follow their own unique way of being.

A counsellor who is not led by their own being – their *daimon* – but instead by trainers and theoretical road maps, is not one who can lead by their listening and can help another person to be led by their own listening. This is a counsellor who is only passively present – present in absence – who refrains from fully presencing their own being and instead listens 'in role'. This is also a frustrating role – hence the endless dispute about how active or directive the counsellor, analysts or psychotherapist should be. Active response to a client is identified with active verbal response or interpretation – rather than with the silent inner activity of listening. Listening is acknowledged as an important activity preceding and prefiguring our verbal response. It is not acknowledged that listening is itself a form of active, wordless and direct response, one that requires us to follow and presence our own being, to be led by its inner voice. If we do so we can also lead a client with the inner voice, and thus not be dependent on our own verbal responses in order to be 'active'. No amount of training in using the 'right' type of words or voice tone in responding to a client can ensure that our verbal and vocal responses are authentic – that they echo the inner voice. Clients are sensitive to the 'who' – not only to the language and character of the counsellor, their voice tone and personality, but also their essential tone of being, their presence. They perceive what the counsellor hears and follows – that is to say, what leads the counsellor. They know intuitively if a counsellor's listening is not led by their own being but merely follows their own verbal-emotional railtracks – or those of the client, or both.

In counselling, as in philosophy, there is always the danger that questions become a substitute for listening and hearing. To bring into view what was un-heard of before means listening to our own questions instead of posing them to others. Philosophical listening seeks to name the common and shared question. Its focus is 'pre-' or 'trans-personal' questions – the relationship between words and the wordless, language and being. Counsellors, on the other hand, listen for personal and inter-personal questions – not questions of Language or Being as such, but the questions of particular human beings – 'clients'. Yet behind a client's words is their whole 'language of being' – their way of listening to, echoing and translating the wordless call of their own being. The essential focus of philosophical counselling, therefore, is not a client's words, body language or silences but their way of responding to the call of their own being – *their way of listening to themselves and others*.

Only by listening to and addressing a client with one's whole being- by silently 'sounding someone out' and not merely echoing or addressing them verbally – are they really 'called', addressed in their very being. What the words of a 'client' or 'patient' essentially reveal or bear forth is not thoughts or feelings, conscious or 'unconscious' but the patience with which they carry or 'bear' themselves pregnantly in silence before speaking – their way of listening or of being called. To attend to a client's way of listening means listening to the process by which they come to speak – how they come to words or words come to them. We can come to speech impatiently – calling things names with habitual or stereotypical words. Or patiently – letting ourselves be really called and touched by the things we name and choosing with care the words we name them with.

The call that calls to the client is the same call that calls to the counsellor – what Heidegger called 'the call of conscience'. The German word for 'conscience' (*Gewissen*) has a meaning closer to 'knowingness'. The call of conscience is a call that "comes from me and yet from beyond me". Heidegger wrote of the way in which we 'listen away from' this call – allowing our inner knowing to get overheard and drowned by everyday discourse and language, by what he called 'idle talk'. But "To let itself get drawn into getting considered and talked about goes against its way of being." The call of conscience "discourses solely and constantly in the mode of keeping silent." To overcome our 'listening away' it must get 'broken off'. "In other words the possibility of another kind of hearing....must be given." To do so the call must first "find itself as something that has failed to hear itself." To be a 'client' is to 'be called' — to be on the way to finding oneself as someone who has failed to hear themselves.

Heidegger's exploration of the meaning of 'conscience', 'guilt', and 'care' are rooted in the idea of the self becoming aware of this failure to hear itself. 'The call' is nothing but the self being silently called to itself and thereby recalled to its "ownmost potentiality for being". Only in responding to this call – in acknowledging its 'guilt' in failing to hear itself, is this guilt transformed into a committed resolve to stay tuned to ourselves and acknowledge the awe-fulness of our potentiality for being. This means being present to ourselves and others in a way which resolves to embrace and presence our entire 'being in time' – the whole of our life's journey, including the anxious foreboding of its end. The 'care' that we embody in so doing is not an 'empathic responsiveness' so much as 'response-ability' – a commitment and capacity to hear which is identical with a constant and honest acknowledgement of 'erring' – of not-hearing. This is not an acknowledgement of 'original sin' but a return to an 'original silence'.

8. The Art of Listening
— 'hearing' and 'hearkening'

We do not understand words because we hear them. What we hear is in large part tuned by our pre-understanding of language, people, contexts and situations. Nor does understanding imply that we have really heard. Understanding what has been said is quite different from the ability to hear and recall the words that were spoken – as is shown by the example of foreign language learners.

If we do not understand a foreign language we hear its words as sounds. Even in our own language we hear words as sounds when we have not (yet) understood them as words. As a result we listen. We listen to speech not in order to hear sounds as sounds but to hear them as words – to understand them. And as soon as we think we understand we stop listening and stop even hearing the words that have been spoken as sounds.

We only begin to listen because there is something lacking or questionable in our understanding – a lack that we need to answer by really hearing. Listening, then, is a form of silent and wordless questioning – a 'questing'. But as soon as we think we understand we are no longer questing, no longer listening. That is why active and prolonged listening is rare. Listening is inseparable from a continuous awareness of not fully hearing and not fully understanding. To maintain our listening means maintaining this continuous sense of not-understanding and not-hearing. That is the meaning of **hearkening**.

Ordinary listening leads to a superficial hearing – one formed by what we already think we understand. **Hearkening** is a type of listening that leads to a deeper more intensive hearing because it is informed and maintained by a continuous sense of not-hearing and not-understanding. **Hearkening** is not hearing but 'not-hearing' – not assuming we have already heard all there is to hear in what we hear. To **hearken** is to be aware of a centre or touchstone of absolute silence within ourselves where we hear nothing. It is by guarding this original silence that we guard our capacity to respond to what calls to us in this silence – not just to respond empathically to others but to hear and caringly awaken each other's 'response-ability' to this call. A response-ability to care for their 'ownmost potentiality for being'.

We hear with the ears. Hearkening means becoming 'all ears', listening with our whole being. We hear sounds and voice tones but we hearken to tones of silence – feeling tones. Paradoxically therefore, our capacity to hearken is like an ability not to hear – to retain an inner silence or deafness even when surrounded by sounds or voices.

"Whatever remains silent divulges nothing. To hear what is silent requires a hearing that each of us has and no-one uses correctly. This hearing (*Gehör*) has something to do not only with the ear, but also with a human's belonging (*Zugehörigkeit*) to what its essence is attuned to. Humans are at-tuned (*ge-stimmt*) to what de-termines (*be-stimmt*) their essence. In this determining humans are touched and called forth by a voice (*Stimme*) that peals all the more purely, the more it silently reverberates through what speaks." (Heidegger)

Hearkening is not just a listening receptivity to this voice, however. It also a way of communicating from it – an 'inner voice communication'. Martin Buber emphasised that it is only in genuinely attuning to and making contact with the inner self of another human being – a 'you' – that we enter a true relation with our own inner being – the eternal 'You'. By itself our inner self is no-self. It's voice is voiceless, except when it speaks to someone and knows whom it is speaking to. We can never 'express' our inner being except by intending and addressing someone from it – intending this 'you' and no other. By intending this person and no other with our listening attention we can also mean something specific with this attention – silently convey specific messages through it.

In sounding out another person with our own essential tone of being we embody and presence our inner being. In this way we also reach out to and contact the inner being of the client. We set up a carrier wave of inner communication on which we both receive and transmit messages through our listening. We not only attune 'empathically' to the multiple voices that we hear in the client's speech and which each of us bear within us. We attune also to an inner voice that belongs to no-one in particular and yet to all, which is neither 'mine' nor 'yours', 'his' nor 'hers', 'ours' nor 'theirs'. This is not the voice of the linguistic 'I' or ego. It is the self experienced as another – not as an 'I' but as a 'you'.

9. The Listening Body
— 'holding' and 'handling'

In a quite tangible way we can 'hold' someone in our gaze. In a similar way we can **hold** someone in our listening attention – in our 'aural gaze'. We become aware of someone **holding** us in their listening when we feel their aural gaze subtly influencing the way we hear ourselves as we speak. **Handling** is the silent modulation tone and touch of our listening gaze, turning it into a carrier wave on which messages are transmitted as well as received.

When we sound people out with our feelings we are also feeling them – touching what I call their listening body. The felt sense we have of someone as they talk to us is not just passive. As we hear them out, our own response begins to gather. As well as being touched, we begin to actively respond to this touch by gently and quietly feeling around. We are feeling with our 'listening body'. And what this feels as it feels around is the listening body of the other. The other person's words are the outer surface or skin of this body, its verbal sheath. Beneath we can register the sensitivity of their listening body, their 'prickliness'. In this way we also sense in advance how they will respond to words and tone of voice which we think of adopting. In doing so we touch them with our listening.

We use our eyes to radiate the tone of our gaze and at the same time to modulate this tone, playing music with subtle eye movements. In this way we 'touch' each other with the tone of our gaze. It is not our physical bodies that touch. And yet to talk of 'touch' here is not a 'mere' metaphor. It is our listening bodies that are in touch 'vibrationally'. Listening is a form of 'inner vibrational touch'. As listeners we touch each other with the tendrils of our intent – the fibres of our listening body.

It is an intrinsic part of many cultures (not least English culture) that this inner touch shall be avoided in communication. As a result people rely solely on probing each other with their words and therefore must do so as sensitively and politely as they can. Handling people by 'sensitively' adjusting our language and tone of voice compensates to a certain degree for handling them through the silent tone and touch of our listening. The alternative – to become mutually conscious of the inner touch involved in listening is threateningly close to the type of intimacy of relating that is associated with close relationships and physical touch. Inner touch is therefore restricted to the therapist's consulting room, in the same way that sex is restricted to the bedroom. This reflects a general social taboo on silence and inner touch, inner **holding** and **handling**. It is this taboo that makes language and verbal communications into totems – charged with symbolic and sexual significance.

One context in which physical touch is permitted outside of sex, albeit with reservations or spurious innuendo – is through therapeutic massage. If massage is to be sensitive and healing it must be more than just a set of mechanical skills or techniques. It must be grounded in the physical attunement of the practitioner, and embody this attunement through a responsive 'listening' to muscle tone and a sensitive **handling** of energy. Similarly, if listening is to be therapeutic it must transcend the intellectual or 'analytic' framework of the listener as well as their immediate emotional reactions. It must be grounded in attunement to feeling tones – embodying these tones in the listener's 'touch' and in their **handling** of the other person.

The word 'analysis' derives from the Greek *analuein* – to loosen or free up. Therapeutic listening and therapeutic massage are both 'analysis' in this essential sense. Therapeutic massage is an art of physical communication or 'messaging' through bodily touch, holding and handling. Its medium is the living tissue of the physical body. The massage practitioner probes gently beneath its skin and loosens the meaningful currents of energy that circulate within tissue. That is perhaps why the Greek word for 'touch' means also 'to kindle'.

Therapeutic listening is itself a form of psychic 'massage' – a form of inner holding and inner handling – a kindling. The listener probes gently beneath the linguistic surface or skin of the listening body to loosen and free the energetic currents of meaning that circulate within and beneath words.

The listening body is like a plant. Its roots grow down into the smallest cavities of our minds and bodies. They infiltrate the inner spaces of our thoughts, and of our very cells. The listening body can send out subtle tendrils of intent. And when we really listen it opens leaves, beckoning their light and warmth.

10. The Discipline of Listening
— 'heeding' and 'with-holding'

'Although this logos holds forever, men fail to comprehend it,
both before hearing it and after they have heard.' (Heraclitus)

Listening is not something we do in between stretches of speaking. It is what we do in order to **heed** someone else's words after they have been spoken and to allow our own response to gather wordlessly before we respond.

"Man is encased in an armour whose task it is to ward off signs." (Buber) The fact that we have heard a person out does not mean that we have taken their words in – **heeded** their unspoken message. To do so we need to delay immediate verbal response and allow a continuing period of silence after we have heard someone out. The more quickly and impatiently we respond to another person's words, the less time we give ourselves to really **heed** them. It is taken for granted in all discussions of counselling skills, that listening involves hearing someone out and not interrupting or foreclosing their speech. If we feel an urge to respond as soon as possible it is difficult to know if we have really heard someone out. Perhaps the person we are listening to has indeed finished speaking – has spoken out all that they wish to say for the time being. This does not mean that we have heard them out. For there is a difference between hearing a person out and hearing their words out. 'Hearing out' means not only hearing out the person and letting them finish. It also means giving ourselves and the speaker time to heed the words that have already been spoken – to let *them* speak to us and reverberate within us.

How long either the counsellor or client talks at any one time – the length of their conversational 'turn' – is not as important as the interval of silence between these turns. It is in this turn interval that the words that have already been spoken can linger in the air and reverberate within us. If we allow them to do so, we hear language speaking – we hear a client's words as the echo of a silent communication of being – the voice of the Between.

The depth of both philosophical dialogue and the counselling conversation are related to the length of the turn interval and to the depth of silence it facilitates. For no matter how short or long people's turns, ordinary conversational patterns, at least in Western culture, reduce the interval of silence *between* turns to an absolute minimum – most often to zero or less than zero. Instead, the turning point of conversation, the point at which the listener begins to speak and the speaker to listen, occurs shortly after – or even before – the speaker has finished speaking. The turning point of our listening, on the other hand, is the point at which our inner listening response to a speaker begins to transform itself into an outward verbal response. If the interval of silence between listening and speaking is minimised, this turning occurs while someone is speaking and therefore before we have given time for their words to resonate within us.

Philosophical counselling demands a fundamental alteration in the timing of our response – re-situating the central turning point of our listening to a point after someone has finished uttering their words. This grants time to take in what has been said and to heed the words that have been used to say it. Only by **with-holding** our verbal and vocal response in this way do we learn to stay in contact and communication with others without speaking – to trust that our own inner response will communicate wordlessly.

The minimalisation of the turn interval in Western culture, not only in everyday conversation but also in philosophical and counselling dialogue, forecloses our listening. It prevents us from experiencing the questing that arises in the gap between language and being. If our thoughts and emotions sometimes reduce us to silence and wordlessness, this silence and wordlessness is not so much 'resistance' to them as an opportunity to listen to ourselves in a new way. It encourages us to find new modes of discourse which not only tolerate but encourage and demand proper periods of silence and wordlessness – time for listening, time for attending to language, time to be and to communicate our being. Time to allow what is gathering within us to speak to us – to 'listen to the logos'. To counsel means to grant time for listening in this way.

The protocol of **with-holding** does not imply that the longer the turn interval the deeper the dialogue. For the physical time that elapses between hearing someone out and giving a response is less important than the psychological time-space that expands within this physical time interval. The physical time interval allows an inward expansion of psychological time – of 'meaning space'. When we give ourselves time to read a book or listen to a piece of music meditatively we also experience an inward expansion of psychological time and allow the meaning space 'between the lines' or 'between the notes' to open up. We open ourselves to the interplay of the outer word and the inner word, the *logos prophorikos* and the *logos endiathetos* – the said and the unsaid.

The unsaid is a common pool of unasked and unanswered questions to which both listener and speaker, both counsellor and client, respond in their thoughts and feelings, their words and gestures. If a counsellor, therapist or analyst 'thinks' something but does not say it, he or she need not be surprised if a client 'picks it up' and articulates it – or vice versa. Instead it has been 'un**said**' – left on the table of silence for the other person to pick up. Perhaps not naming or describing it in our terms, but in their own. In not expressing a thought aloud, the latter does not disappear, nor is it telepathically transmitted verbatim. It communicates through the silent tone of our listening.

Listening always involves 'unsaying' – leaving things unsaid. Speaking is a response to the unsaid. Language the tool with which we name it. To **hint** at the unsaid in implicit language is like pointing to what is there between us on this table or altar of silence. Describing it in language that is too explicit can be like picking an object up from this table – or even wresting it out of the other person's hands – and brandishing it. Language that is merely explicit leaves the table emptied, the silence bare. Meaning then evaporates. Conversely, to leave something unsaid – to 'withhold' a particular thought, feeling, or interpretation – can mean that I let it rest in the silence between us, or that I cover and conceal it in words. Yet there is a third way of withholding – a genuine **with-holding.** This means holding the object on the table with the other person, hand on hand – helping them to feel safe in **handling** it by handling it with them.

Silence can be threatening because the objects on the altar of silence are threatening, because I fear to look at them, hold or handle them psychically. It can also be threatening because I wish to hide them in silence, fearing they may otherwise be mis-interpreted, lost to me or substituted with other objects. I can fear so much that I allow nothing to appear on the table, try to wipe it clear or cover it with a verbal tablecloth. The silence that opens up when a counsellor **with-holds** immediate response and allows an interval of silence can be threatening because it exposes this table. It is made safe by **with-holding** – by holding and handling its objects together. What are these objects? They are not things, nor even thoughts and feelings. They are our silent and unstated questions. **With-holding** means **holding** and **handling** these unstated question with a speaker, questing with them rather than answering their questions for them or posing questions to them. It does not mean that we withdraw aloofly into ourselves. What we hold back is only a premature outward response – verbal or physical. This gives us a chance to **heed** a person's words and **hearken** to the silent questing of their being.

With-holding automatically sets a tone 'at variance' with the client's own way of listening and responding. The interplay of client and counsellor is a dialogue between contrasting ways of listening, two approaches to the timing of dialogical response and exchange. The client may be unsettled by the silence occasioned by the counsellor's **with-holding** of immediate responses, and continue to respond themselves without any interval of silence whenever the counsellor has spoken. In such a case the counsellor cannot immediately seek to slow the tempo of dialogical exchange, but must gradually introduce longer pauses and periods of **with-**

holding. The manner of doing so also embodies the counsellor's **handling** of the client and of the questions they raise.

The protocol of **with-holding** carries the same significance in philosophical counselling as the basic rule of so-called 'free association' in psychoanalysis – that the analysand should speak whatever comes into their minds. **With-holding** is in a certain sense a contrary principle, suggesting that we should give time for impressions to gather force within us (*legein*) before translating these impressions into words or images. It applies in the first place to counsellors themselves, providing them not only with the time-space necessary to really **heed** a client's words, but with a parameter by which to gauge the quality and patience of the client's own listening – their capacity to **with-hold** and **heed**.

In psychoanalysis, silence on the part of the client may be interpreted as a form of resistance. In philosophical counselling the only 'resistance' is resistance to silence – to allowing ourselves to 'pause for thought' and listen inwardly. Personality is the way we bear ourselves forth in speech. Character is the way we *bear ourselves in silence*. The focus of philosophical counselling is the character of a client's listening, the *inner bearing* of their silence. This is reflected in body language. The more uncomfortable we are with silence, the more this shows itself in our posture. The discomfort expresses an incapacity to *be* and to *embody* our being in silence. We cannot really be with others in silence unless we can 'bear' ourselves in this silence. This means finding an inner bearing and posture through which we can both stay in contact with our selves and be with others. In speech we often engage in contact with others whilst at the same losing contact with ourselves. In listening we often do the reverse. **With-holding** provides an opportunity to learn how to be in silence – to find our bearings psychically and physically. Our body language in silence reveals the tension between psychically withdrawing and physically presencing ourselves, being with ourselves and being with others, listening inwardly and listening outwardly.

To listen means to 'list' or lean. When we listen we lean inwardly towards another with our whole being. The listing of the listener cannot be reduced to 'body language'. To 'lean towards another with an open posture' as instructed by manuals on listening and body language is no guarantee that we are really listening – merely that we are giving the physical appearance of listening. It is our inner bearing and posture as listeners that is the basis of our intellectual positions, our emotional stances, and our physical posture itself, of our whole way of speaking. This inner bearing is our inner relation to both being and language, manifest in the way we **hearken** and **heed.** The essential bearing of the Philosophical Counsellor – that of **with-holding** – is not merely an outward stance of holding back and keeping silent but an inner one: "We understand only too well that a thinker would prefer to hold back the word that is to be said, not in order to keep it for himself, but to bear it towards the encounter with what is to be thought." (Heidegger) This stance does not imply that we abandon the quest for words that can name and describe the wordless impressions that gather within us as we listen. Listening is also a wordless quest for the naming words. **With-holding** is a stance which respects the essential paradox of this quest.

"How is he to give a name to what he is still questing for?
To assign the naming word is after all, what constitutes finding."

11. The Protocols of Philosophical Counselling — the 'listening circle'

In a group context the principle of **with-holding** can be formalised in what I call a Listening Circle. Two basic ground rules or protocols are necessary to establish a Listening Circle. These are also the basic protocols of Philosophical Counselling, providing a framework of interaction that encourages a Listening Dialogue.

Protocol 1

The first protocol is that no participant in the group shall respond immediately to another, but shall instead allow a variable period of silence – a 'turn interval' in which to **heed** and **hearken**.

Protocol 2

The second protocol is that no participant shall address their questions or statements directly to another member of the group. This protocol helps people

(a) to communicate by **hinting** – to intend a message for another person inwardly, indirectly and implicitly rather than outwardly, directly and explicitly,

(b) to **heed** their own questions – questions they would usually pass on by addressing them to a another member of the group and challenging that person to answer for them.

By **with-holding** from direct questioning they open themselves instead to receive an answering call from their own being – or from the group. For as each person's words linger in silence, others can also **heed** them – hear them as responses to their own wordless or unspoken questions, as bearers of a message from themselves.

Many counsellors are trained to communicate through explicit statements and questions. Communication that is entirely explicit, however, is effectively meaningless – it lacks an inner logos – the *logos endiathetos*. Entirely explicit statements conceal the inner questing of our being, they carry no questioning undertone. By **hearkening** to and **heeding** the implicit messages borne by speech (including their own) participants can also learn to speak in a more sensitive and conscious way – to hint. **Hinting** means asking questions that say something from ourselves, and making statements which implicitly address and question other members of the group. It is the philosopher counsellor's function to teach the language of hinting, to transform the word into a bearer of an inner message, an act of un-saying. This is in one sense a paradoxical strategy, for as Heidegger noted: "To hear a hint, one must first...hear oneself into the region from which it comes." It is by the practice of **with-holding** that this region also opens itself to our hearing, often in a quite striking and dramatic way. Experiencing an extended silence in the turn-interval people begin to hear *under* language. After taking part in a Listening Circle they begin to recognise in retrospect the superficiality of discussions characterised by rapid verbal exchange in which the pregnancy of silence is aborted or miscarried in speech.

The Listening Circle is the 'experiential' basis of education in Philosophical Counselling. Its 'theoretical' basis is a philosophy of listening and of counselling. Experiential and theoretical education are not separated but interwoven both theoretically and experientially. All philosophical dialogue concerning 'theoretical' issues becomes 'experiential' when it is conducted under the protocols of the Listening Circle. These can also be formalised in a one-to-one setting – treating it as a group of two, and transforming discussion into a Listening Dialogue. Through a Listening Dialogue one-to-one tutoring in philosophy ceases to be merely academic or theoretical and becomes a form of 'mentoring'-philosophy as counselling and counselling as philosophy. The tutor responds to the student neither as an academic philosopher nor as personal counsellor but as a philosophical counsellor and mentor – modelling and embodying a new way of listening.

The basic stance of the philosophical counsellor acknowledges that all questions are fundamentally shared questions, questions that arise in the ever-present gap between language and being.

This stance can only be maintained if it is reflected in a different way of speaking – a speaking grounded in listening. Whenever a philosophical counsellor listens to people speak about something, he or she must be aware of what they are saying to each other, to the group, or to the counsellor – even though their remarks might in no way be explicitly intended, addressed to or mean another person. This does not imply that the counsellor should interpret implicit meanings in words, like an individual or group analyst. The point is not to interpret implicit meanings in words (to make them explicit) but to receive and respond to them on the same level – wordlessly and implicitly. The counsellor must be aware of language as the metaphor of an ongoing and silent dialogue of being – and participate in this dialogue. This means two things: responding silently from their own being to the language of the other person, and responding with their own language and not borrowed ways of speaking to the being of the other.

To be a philosopher is to think. This means to be a listener. To be a listener means being able to fully **be** in silence with another. Not to depend on language and speech in order to actively presence one's own being. The 'authority' of the counsellor is the authenticity of their own *language of being* and their own listening responsiveness to the client's language of being. The vocation of the counsellor is to *be* (in) *listening* – thereby to **hearken** to what calls to us from another human being. This is not so much a role as an inner vocation shared by all – for to have a vocation is to respond to a calling.

Philosophical counselling is not linked to particular professional or theoretical languages. Its 'theoretical' focus is the nature of language and being. Its 'practical' focus is the client's characteristic way of listening to and translating their own language of being. The way we word our own experience reflects our listening self-consciousness of language – our capacity to speak our own being and to discriminate between its voice and the voices of language. At the same time 'wording is worlding'. Our way of 'being in the world' embodies our way of 'being in the word' – of dwelling in the meaning space housed by language.

This meaning space is more than just the semantics of words. It includes the meaningful psychic interiority of our own bodies and the meaningful psychic exteriority of the bodies around us – the people, objects and events of our world.

The proliferating schools of psychoanalysis, counselling and therapy each compete to assert the universality and truth of their own theoretical languages. Philosophy grounds our understanding of all these languages in the native language of the psyche – the language of inner tonality or resonance. Philosophical listening is meditative listening – a deeper way of hearing and under-standing the vocabularies employed by both clients and professional helpers themselves. The point is not to rely on any theoretical perspectives as a touchstone for our listening but to find an inner touchstone – the inner voice. And yet to develop an adequate philosophy of listening means also finding a language by which to describe the inner activity of listening.

Hearkening, holding, handling, heeding, with-holding and **hinting** are some of the basic elements of this language of listening, its philosophical and experiential keywords. Learning to counsel philosophically means learning what these keywords really mean in practice. Education in philosophical counselling involves introducing the keywords to others in a thoughtful and living way. This is achieved not through writing, speaking or intellectual discussion alone – through talking about the keywords, but through a mode of discourse which at the same time embodies them – the Listening Circle and its protocols. For we cannot discuss the subject of listening deeply unless we are at the same time listening and seeking to deepen that listening.

A Listening Dialogue cannot be reduced to verbal communication, non-verbal body language, emotional expression or intellectual discussion. 'Talking about' and 'expressing' are aspects of communication. A Listening Dialogue **hearkens** to the intercourse of being that underlies verbal communication. From this **hearkening** it seeks to name what it is that the verbal communication itself is essentially 'about'. In 'On the Way to Language' Heidegger presents 'A Dialogue on Language' with a

Japanese interlocutor. In the course of this dialogue he mentions his conversations with a certain Count Kuki:

"Our dialogues were not formal, scholarly discussions. Whenever that sort of thing seemed to be taking place, Count Kuki remained silent...They made the Eastasian world more luminously present, and the dangers of our dialogues became more clearly visible."

The danger in question was that of trying to talk about Eastasian art and poetry in European terms, and that in this process "the language of the dialogue constantly destroyed the possibility of saying what the dialogue was about." This is a danger that attends all counselling and therapeutic conversations. And yet it is our very awareness of it that can transform such conversation into a Listening Dialogue.

12. Going on Being — Heidegger and Winnicott

In his essay 'On Communication' Winnicott wrote of the healthy use of 'active non-communication' for the purpose of 'feeling real', as opposed to communication that expresses the compliant behaviour of a 'false self'. Notably, he describes this false self as born of an early interference in just 'going on being'.

Compliance can be expressed in the very act of speaking, irrespective of content, which may be a denial of our freedom to dwell silently within the reality of our own being and hearken to its tones. Compliance can also manifest itself in speech as role compliance – using the 'right' words and phrases, the 'right' register or emotional vocabulary. Equally, compliance may govern our way of listening – adopting the 'right' tone of voice and body posture, asking the 'right' sort of questions. Then we are no longer listening with our whole being, but listening in role – listening as a counsellor, as an analyst, as a parent, friend or helper.

Uniquely amongst psychoanalytic thinkers, Winnicott, like Heidegger, used a language that spoke of being. "After being, doing and being done to. But first, being." He spoke of the mother's **holding** of the infant as "keeping the baby safe from unpredictable and therefore traumatic events that interrupt going-on-being". Going-on-being is contrasted with environmental unreliability, the need to react to external 'impingements' and the threat of annihilation:

"In this place which is characterised by the essential existence of a holding environment, the 'inherited potential' (of the infant) is becoming a 'continuity of being'. The alternative to being is reacting, and reacting interrupts being and annihilates. Being and annihilation are the two alternatives. The holding environment therefore has as its main function the reduction to a minimum of impingements to which the infant must react with resultant annihilation of personal being."

Winnicott also speaks of the mother's **handling** of the infant. "Handling describes the environmental provision that corresponds roughly with the establishment of a psycho-somatic partnership". Through her careful handling of the infant's body, the infant's psyche feels able to dwell safely within its body. Winnicott emphasises the importance of this 'indwelling' to the infant's sense of 'going-on-being'.

The word infant derives from the Latin *in-fans*: not-speaking. As we acquire language we learn to handle and protect ourselves with words. The mother tongue replaces the mother. But the transition to verbal communication often goes hand in hand, not only with the gradual separation of mother and child, but with a growing rift between language and being. Winnicott described this rift as the splitting off of an intellectual 'false self' from the psyche-soma. The latter remains the location of a 'true self', but one that has now become an incommunicable core.

Winnicott implies that psychopathology is in some way a result of failures in environmental provision – of adequate **holding** and **handling**. Heidegger, on the other hand, saw the schizoid rift between language and being not as the exceptional result of personal upbringing, but as the ruling framework of our technical-industrial world. Such is the rift between language and being that characterises the media-, market- and technology driven society that the therapeutic listening demanded by so-called 'depressive', 'schizophrenic' or 'borderline' individuals is not simply a response to an individual pathology but to a social one. Mental illness challenges us to acknowledge the absence or foreclosure of real listening in social life. To remedy this absence we can only start with ourselves, by removing the barriers that prevent us from really listening with our whole being.

"There are many, many people living in private dungeons today, people who give no evidence of it whatever on the outside, where you have to listen very sharply to hear the faint message from the dungeon." (Rogers)

Winnicott saw a reparative role for psychoanalysis. Heidegger saw a reparative role for philosophy in restoring the link between language and being. Whereas for Winnicott, as for Freud, psychoanalysis was a 'talking cure', for Heidegger philosophical thinking was a 'listening cure' – linked in its very essence to the way we hear language, hear each other and respond to the call of our own being. Those trapped in the dungeon are not simply not heard, they are also not listening. The way we were listened to as infants and children has no doubt a great influence on our capacity to listen to ourselves. But no matter how little we were heard in our early years, one way that we can overcome the psychological deformations or disturbances that may have resulted is by learning to listen to others. Perhaps this is one of the things that lead people to want to train as counsellors. Perhaps also one of the key desires of the client in counselling is not simply to be heard, but to learn to listen and hear. It is through learning to listen to others that we learn to hear ourselves just as it is through learning to hear ourselves that we learn to listen to others.

Significantly, Winnicott speaks of the analyst **holding** the patient by "conveying *in words* [my stress] at the appropriate moment something that shows that the analyst knows and understands the deepest anxiety that is being experienced or that is waiting to be experienced." And yet just as the mother's way of physically holding and handling the infant depends on her sensitivity to the infant, so the way we handle ourselves and others in speech depends on how we come to words or they to us – depends on the way we listen.

The importance of a philosophy and psychology of listening is constantly obscured by the false controversy over whether mental illness is 'caused' by environmental or genetic factors, a debate which conceals the true genealogy of character. 'Genealogy' implies speaking about the way things come to be – their genesis. The way we speak about how things come to be affects the way they come to be. The genealogy of character is the way we each come to be who we are *dia-logos* – through the word. This depends both on our acquired language and the thought patterns these embody, and on the way we listen. Our way of listening determines how we 'think' – how we choose words and how we hear and respond to them. This also affects how we respond to our genetic inheritance.

Proponents of genetic 'causality' may admit that environmental factors influence whether particular genes will manifest in physical or mental illness, just as proponents of environmental causality may admit that genetic factors may affect our response to environmental impingements. Yet whilst both geneticists and environmentalists use their own biological, sociological or psychological languages to explain psychopathology it is paradoxical that neither acknowledges the role of language as such in the life of the individual and society. Language shapes the way we interpret and respond to both our own genetic inheritance and to our environmental or social inheritance. The task of philosophy is to remind us that we cannot explain things in scientific, psychiatric or psychoanalytic terms unless we question what it is that we are seeking to explain with it. To talk, for example about the 'causes' of 'schizophrenia' or 'depression' assumes that we know what it is that these terms name. To say that they 'categorise groups of symptoms' does not mean that they are based on empirical facts – for symptoms themselves are described and interpreted in words. We forget that both words were coined within the last two centuries. Are we to assume that because a word such as 'depression' has a contemporary or 'scientific' ring it is better than older ones such as 'melancholy'?

The genealogy of mental illness has as much do with the way in which society comes to use terms such as 'stress' and 'depression' as it does with the way in which individuals come to handle and shape their self-experience in words. The individual and social dimensions of wording are intimately connected. For it is when the language of everyday discourse fails the individual that he or she takes recourse to forms of speech and communication that appear 'pathological'. This is mirrored in the way society itself takes recourse to the language of pathology – to medical, psychiatric and psychoanalytic terminologies. Such institutionalised modes of discourse often bear within them the same 'schizoid', or 'paranoid' pathology that confronts society in the patient. The language of 'psychopathology' in other words, to some degree embodies the very pathologies it describes. A classic example is the writings of Melanie Klein, imbued as they are with a paranoid tone.

For Heidegger the essence of all 'pathology' was *forgetfulness of being.*. This is mirrored in a forgetfulness of language and its history. Heidegger used etymology to challenge this linguistic amnesia – to remind us, for example, that the word 'logic' derives from the Greek *logos*. If we listen to the word 'genealogy' in a similar way we can hear it speaking not about the genesis of things but about the genesis of speech and of the word – *logos*. The word 'Genealogy' also says 'logogenesis'. 'Genealogy' – the way we come to be, and 'logogenesis' – the way the word comes to be are one. We come to be who we are through the word and we come to the word from who we are. The way we do so is the way we listen. Listening re-links the language and being through what Winnicott called the psyche-soma – with our wordless and felt sense of meaning. This is composed of those wavelengths of attunement that constitute 'feeling tone'. They are the inner resonance or logos of the psyche. They are also its pathos – the basis of 'empathy' and 'telepathy' as well as of 'pathology'. A philosophical understanding of 'pathology' rooted in etymology pays heed to logogenesis (the coming to be of the word) and etymo-logy (the truth of the word) in a quite different way to either psychoanalysis or academic philology. A philosophical psychiatry would need to pay heed to the nature of listening in a deeper way than either psychoanalysis or conventional counselling. To understand it as a form of silent 'telepathic' as well as 'empathic communication'. Winnicott himself distinguished between what he called explicit and indirect communication – including verbal communication – and something that he termed 'silent communication'. He saw the latter as an attempt to restore a sense of reality – of being one's real self, and yet he denied its inter-personal reality, regarding it as a communication with personal and 'subjective objects' only.

"Here communication is not non-verbal; it is, like the music of the spheres, absolutely personal. It belongs to being alive....The two extremes, explicit communication that is indirect, and silent or personal communication that feels real, each of these has its place, and in the intermediate cultural area there exists for many, but not for all, a mode of communication which is a most valuable compromise."

The analogy with 'the music of the spheres' is a telling one. When we listen to someone speak there is a sense in which we hear them play their own music. Their words are not their music but an interpretation of it – like lyrics put to a melody. Their voices are not their music but their way of singing these lyrics. Their body language is not their music, but their way of playing this music – of embodying it. The images that this music generates in us are not the music but our way of dreaming it. Music is not word, images, gesture or sound. We hearken to music not as sound but through sound. We do so through sounds of silence – through feeling tone. We hear each other's music as a silent music – the music of feeling tone, the music of being. We respond to it not only with words but from our being. We respond silently and wordlessly – musically.

Two composers working with equal skill and care will not produce the same type of music. Two mothers giving their infants the same degree of care (or lack of it) will not affect the infant in the same way. And neither would two analysts – even were they able to listen from the exactly same theoretical perspective – mean the same thing to a given client. Nor would two clients mean the same thing to a therapist, even if their modes of relating were similar and they seemed to affect the therapist in a similar way through a similar type of 'transference'. Irrespective of 'transference', people mean something to us by virtue of who they are – their 'language of being'. This may or may not be embedded in disturbed or disturbing features of language and speech, character and personality. One must appreciate a composer's music intimately, however, in order to really hear the way in which a conductor or performer is interpreting and shaping this music through their personality and character – to hear the way they are hearing it – or not hearing it.

The infant is in thrall to the mother's 'performance'. And yet the way she handles the infant is not her music but her playing of this music. This playing can be mechanical and erratic or sensitively attuned – musical. If it is musical then it is based not simply on a listening receptivity to her own being, but on a sensitive attunement to the 'music' of the infant – its language of being. Then the music that is played is not hers alone but a common music. The music of what Buber called the Between. Wording is a type of handling comparable to mothering. Wording is the handling and shaping of our pre-verbal, bodily or 'musical' sense of meaning. This felt sense is attuned to the Between. In listening to people's language, therefore, we hear not only the way they handle themselves and others in speech, but the nature of their listening attunement to this Between – their way of hearing and playing its music.

The inter-personal reality of silent communication is easily experienced. Talking to someone on the phone we receive no body signals and yet, irrespective of the frequency or tone of their vocal responses, we can sense if they are genuinely listening. If at some point they 'turn off' – become bored or impatient, we 'hear' it in the tones of their silence. This is a type of hearing that can also tell us if someone is still listening to themselves as they speak – still attuned to the call that 'comes from me and yet from beyond me'.

13. Philosophical Restraint and the Act of Faith — Heidegger and Bion

Both philosophy and psychoanalysis involve a fundamental questioning of language – listening for a reality 'beneath' or 'behind' people's words and beneath or behind the language of sensuous experience. Bion frequently warned of the danger of anticipating the nature of this pre- or trans-verbal dimension in terms of familiar psychoanalytic theory and its terminologies. Similarly, Heidegger warned of the danger of representing it in the conventional 'metaphysical' language of philosophy. By this he meant talking 'about' it instead of talking from it, discoursing on truth instead of *telling* the truth, posing abstract verbal questions instead of questioning language from a position under or beneath it.

What Freud called 'the unconscious' can be seen as an underside or 'other side' of language. The unconscious is in this sense a 'consciousness of the Un-', one demanding a capacity to bear the terrors and wonder of the un-familiar, the un-known and the un-canny. Here words do not represent things. Nor can their meaning simply be defined in other words. Nor can meaning be reduced either to an extra-psychic reality or to a linguistic system or network of signifiers. The meaning of a word is not a thing or a word – it is an un-word and an un-thing.

The word not does not capture a thought so much as point to something still un-thought – a word-less and silent knowing that transcends language and sensuous experience. It requires an especially disciplined listening to hearken to the 'unthought'. Heidegger sought to define this basic discipline or inner disposition – one that the philosopher must embody as an individual and not merely define or describe.

"If we had to say something about this basic disposition of philosophy,...we might call it 'restraint' (*Verhaltenheit*). In it, two elements belong together and are as one: terror in the face of what is closest and most obtrusive, namely that beings are, and awe in the face of what is remotest, namely that in beings, and before each being, Being holds sway. Restraint is the disposition in which this terror is not overcome and set aside but is precisely preserved and conserved through awe. Restraint is the basic disposition of the relation to Being, and in it the concealment of the essence of Being becomes what is most worthy of questioning."

It was W.R. Bion who likewise attempted to define psychoanalysis, not as a mere theory of the mind, but as a way of listening based on a particular disposition or discipline. In describing this discipline Bion refers to what Keats called Negative Capability: "..that is, when a man is capable of being in uncertainties, mysteries, doubts without any irritable reaching after fact and reason."

Just as Heidegger distinguishes constantly between empirical beings and Being, Bion emphasises the distinction between sensuous and non-sensuous reality. Knowledge and language derived from sensuous experience he signifies by the sign 'K'. The analyst on the other hand "must focus his attention on 'O', the unknown and unknowable." Here the sign 'O' points, I believe, to the same essential reality which Heidegger refers to as 'the truth of Being'.

"Every object known or knowable by man, including himself, must be an evolution of O....The psychoanalyst can know what the patient says, does and appears to be, but cannot know the O of which the patient is an evolution: he can only 'be' it. He knows phenomena by virtue of his senses but, since his concern is with O, events must be regarded as possessing either the defects of irrelevancies obstructing, or the merits of pointers initiating, the process of 'becoming' O."

The *Verhaltenheit* which Heidegger speaks of and which is usually translated as 'restraint' is what I have linked with the process of listening and call 'with-holding'. This bears comparison with the 'negative capability' which Bion describes using the signs 'K' and 'O'.

"A fallacious but helpful description is that....the analyst must wait for the analytic session to 'evolve'. He must wait not for the analysand to talk or to be silent or to gesture, or for any other occurrence that is an actual event, but for an evolution to take place so that O becomes manifest in K through the emergence of actual events."

We cannot reach what Bion calls 'at one-ment' with O from K – from sensuous knowledge and experience. Instead we can only wait for an event of transformation to occur in O. Such events do not occur 'in' us but in the 'between'. "The interpretation is an actual event in O that is common to analyst and analysand." Whereas Heidegger speaks of the philosopher's 'restraint', Bion refers to the negative capability of the analyst as 'act of faith' (F). Only through this act of faith can the analyst transcend sensuous knowledge (K) and become open to a direct cognition of O through 'at-one-ment' – not a knowing 'about' but a knowing inseparable from being. The act of faith hinges on a 'disciplined denial' of desire, memory and understanding, all of which are aspects of K. For "if the mind is preoccupied with elements perceptible to sense, it will be much less able to perceive elements that cannot be sensed."

What is this 'non-sensuous' reality or 'essential truth of Being', why is it so important and how can it possibly be represented if not in sensuously derived language? This is a question which both Bion and Heidegger address. In doing so they both pose questions concerning the very nature of thinking Heidegger does so from a 'philosophical' standpoint, arguing that the essence of thinking can in no way be reduced to the representation of truth in words and images. But if there is another dimension to thinking besides representation what is it?

For Bion, the other dimension of thinking is 'hallucination'. Bion is not here referring to visual or auditory 'hallucinations' in the ordinary sense – apparitions identical in nature to sensuously perceptible objects or voices. Nor is he even referring to dreams or to dreamlike images. "...hallucinations are not representations: they are things in themselves born of intolerance of frustration and desire."

Here Bion alludes to his psychoanalytic theory of thinking, deriving from Freud and Klein. According to this theory the capacity for verbal representation and thinking depends on the infant's capacity to tolerate the loss of the breast, to allow the word to replace the thing, the mother tongue to replace the mother. Psychotic speech and 'thinking' however, is based on a different relationship to language, one which stems from an incapacity to tolerate the pain and frustration of loss. This generates a way of thinking in which words symbolise 'hallucinatory' internal objects which transcend representation in words or images. Instead they are 'evacuated' through the senses and 'projected' into real people or objects. These internal objects are not real things or representations of real things and yet they are real for the psychotic. They are 'un-things' or 'no-things'.

"The patient feels the pain of an absence of fulfilment of his desires. The absent fulfilment is experienced as a no-thing. The emotion aroused by the 'no-thing' is felt as indistinguishable from the 'no-thing'. The emotion is replaced by a 'no-emotion'. In practice this can mean no feeling at all, or an emotion such as rage....that is, an emotion of which the fundamental function is a denial of another emotion."

In language resonant with the central themes of Heidegger's 'Being and Time', Bion used clinical material to describe how references to past and future in the language of the psychotic represent "the place where the present used to be".

"The 'place' where time was (or a feeling was, or a 'no-thing' of any kind was, is then similarly annihilated. There is thus created a domain of the non-existent."

Bion seeks to explicitly differentiate this psychoanalytic account of the difference between psychotic and non-psychotic thinking from a philosophical understanding:

"...the word representing a thought is not the same as the identical word when it is representing an hallucination. The difference between philosophy (and even theoretical psychoanalysis) and the practice of psychoanalysis can be seen by considering what the detection of this difference means for the philosopher or theoretician and what it means for the practicing psychoanalyst who has to decide in the emotional situation itself whether the patient's statements represent an hallucination or a fact of external reality. It is for this reason that the psychoanalyst must be experienced in non-sensuous realities and able to ignore sensuously derived experience..."

If I have quoted Bion at some length it is in order to be able to now bring out in more depth some of the important parallels and contrasts between a philosophical and a psychoanalytic understanding of thinking, and of 'hallucination' and 'psychosis'.

The ground on which we dwell is not a pre-given rational, linguistic or scientific structure. Nor do beings exist simply in order to serve in some human or divine purposes. Time is not there to be used. People are not bundles of skills to be exploited. The earth is more than a stock of industrial resources. The ground of reason itself is Being – and Being requires no rational-intellectual justification. And yet we dwell within the meaning space of language as we dwell within the world. If our relationship to language – our way of 'being in the word' – is dominated by calculative thinking, by 'rational' projects and purposes, our 'being in the world' will be characterised by intellectual, emotional and physical *ungroundedness* – from 'forgetfulness of Being'. The less grounded we are in our Being, the less we feel at home in the world and the more we cling to intellectual, professional, ethnic and cultural identities. Political, economic, ethnic and familial insecurity however, all ensure that not everyone achieves the safety of a secure but social 'identity' or 'ego'. The individual 'unconscious' is an *under-conscious* – threatening social ego-identity in the same way that the 'under-class' threatens the respectable citizen or the under-developed countries threaten the developed world.

Migrants, refugees and Jews have all symbolised the rootless, homeless wandering element of the soul, the element whom life itself forces to become more familiar with the under-world of consciousness. This is the often turbulent under-consciousness of society and of the individual. 'Going under' in this way is difficult.

And yet it is this under-world and under-consciousness that is at the same time the source of all language, thought and creativity.

The word 'hallucination' derives from the Greek *aluein* – to wander or roam restlessly. If our consciousness wanders it does not represent to itself in advance where it goes or where it will find itself. In this sense hallucination is akin to true listening. It belongs to the essence of listening that we do not represent in advance what we will hear. That does not mean that we do not anticipate at all, for we cannot be truly present to ourselves and others except by 'anticipating' – by bearing ourselves towards that which comes to meet us from the 'future'. We cannot sense meaning except by opening our 'sixth sense' – that sense of meaning which comes about because we also mean the other person, intend them with our being and are meaningful for them.

Philosophically, it is listening which is the other dimension of thinking, its wordless and non-representational dimension. Through listening (*Zuhören*) we ground ourselves and our identity in the 'beneath' as a 'between' – in a mutual belonging (*Zugehörigkeit*) to each other and to Being. Listening too, is a 'negative capability', a capacity to roam and find our bearings in new territory – despite our un-certainty and despite its un-familiarity or un-canniness.

Without this negative capability however, the homeless wandering of the under-class and under-consciousness may indeed take other, 'psychotic' forms. Bion makes use of the paradigm of 'container' and 'contained' to describe the relationship between 'K' and 'O', word and meaning – 'language' and 'being'. We need not only words and representational thinking but our own and each other's listening as a 'container' for our own word-less meanings and for the affirmation of our own essential being.

Without a *listening culture* and a *listening ethics* society is condemned to an on-going conflict between an ungrounded 'rational' sanity on the one hand and inexpressible and unheard suffering on the other. In this situation some make a career as analysts and others as 'neurotics' or 'psychotics'. Some live a life of 'successful' normality, and others a life that 'goes under' through social and psychological breakdown. Psychoanalysis should provide an opportunity for these two poles of society to meet, allowing those who seek to become genuine listeners to encounter those who go under – who fail to keep their heads high and 'above water'. The latter embody the 'under-consciousness' of normal society – one that it insistently fails to hear. The type of listening that this encounter demands is not ordinary or 'normal'. Both philosophical thinking, in Heidegger's sense, and psychoanalytic listening in the sense described by Bion, open us to a socially abnormal depth of 'hearing'. To talk about this type of grounded thinking or listening in words is difficult. But it is hinted at by the term *Daseinsanalytik*, one used to refer to a philosophically-oriented psychiatry and psychoanalysis deriving from Heidegger and developed by Medard Boss.

Dasein can be literally translated as 'being there'. The sense which I wish to suggest for the term *Daseinsanalytik* is one that is a reversal of Freud's principle that *there* where the 'id' *was* the 'ego' shall *be*. It means taking listening as the opportunity to liberate thinking from the ego and verbal representation and to ground it in the wordless reality of our being – to be there where ego is not. This is the place where experience is suffered not represented, interpreted and contained by language. Instead we contain it. We hear – not the ear, and not the mind. The self that hears in this way is not the speaking self – the language mind or the voice persona. It is the 'listening self' – our listening being.

14. Being's Withdrawal
— the deconstruction of 'depression'

The *Da* of Heidegger's term *Dasein* is reminiscent of the 'Fort...Da' ('gone..there') of Freud – the language game by which an infant represented the alternating presence and absence of its mother by repetitively discarding and retrieving an object. The experience of loss, absence and mourning holds an important if not central place in Kleinian theory of psychological development as it does in the developmental psychology deriving from Bowlby. For Heidegger, the essence of loss is in no way reducible to any psychological processes, but is to do with what he calls the 'abandonment of beings by Being' or Being's 'withdrawal'. A psychoanalyst might be tempted to interpret such obscure and yet high-flown philosophical language as a mere metaphor of the philosopher's 'depression', originating in a primal experience of withdrawal or loss of the breast. In this chapter I wish to show how, on the contrary, it is Heidegger's language that can illuminate in a new way both the psychoanalytic understanding of loss and the entire psychological vocabulary of emotional states, neurotic and psychotic – in particular common terms such as anxiety, paranoia and depression.

Whereas for Freud the human ego is suspended between 'id' and 'super-ego' for Heidegger human being – *Dasein* – is constituted by its own paradoxical relation to Being as such. The primordial need and distress of human beings (both represented by the German word *Not*) are rooted not in the physical and emotional needs of the infant and the ways these are met or not met, but in the fundamental character of our age, which conceals a more essential *Not* . The characteristic of this need and distress is that its very existence as a need is denied or dismissed. This is the need and desire to be, that is to say – re-find the ground of our human thinking, feeling and willing in the wonder, depth and darkness of our own Being rather than in reason or emotion, facts or phantasy, technologies or psychologies, mechanism or sexuality.

"Everything becomes obvious, without any impenetrable depths, and this transparency derives from a luminosity in which the eye of knowledge is dazzled to the verge of blindness...And it is a gaping abyss that beings, apparently closer to reality than ever before, can be taken for all that is, while Being and the truth of Being are forgotten."

The need and distress, the abyss and the abandonment that Heidegger speaks of are seen as an unproductive, dark, and negative side of human nature that is to be overcome by 'positive mental attitude', 'rational-emotive' coping, psychiatric treatment or manipulative self-management, self-help and self-programming. When such rational self-management proves inadequate it is experienced as an unproductive sickness – as 'mental illness'. This in turn is put down to any number of external or internal factors, reasons or causes, except the most fundamental – the *pull of the ground*.

The human being is suspended between the pull of the ground and the dominant commercial and technological framework of human society – what Heidegger called The Frame (*Gestell*). The different emotional states that people find themselves in are ways in which we experience this suspension and respond to the pull of the ground. People speak of feeling 'down', or worse, of the 'black hole' of depression. A black hole, as we know from cosmology, is a concentration of matter so great that it collapses in on itself and its enormous gravity prevents any light from escaping. We associate depression with darkness, silence, heaviness and with psychological compression, confusion and implosion. These are all ways in which we experience the pull of the ground – but only if we fear and resist this pull. It takes enormous effort and work to resist the pull of our own depths – the gravitational pull exerted by the invisible core of the human being. Some use work to avoid feeling it. Others experience the anxiety of our oscillating suspension that is caught between the Frame and the pull of the ground, between Reason and Being. Science and calculation seek in reason the ground of all things, as if beings could have a reason or purpose without first being. We believe either that our existence is something we need to ground in reason – explain or justify by facts or by our human purposes, or that it is essentially groundless, purposeless and meaningless.

Work, the accumulation of commodities, money, power and status, as well as entertainment, sex, drugs and alcohol offer means of avoiding the pull of the ground. With them our essential Being withdraws into its depths. That is why without them people feel 'withdrawal' symptoms – restlessness, lack of concentration and 'depression' – for they become conscious of how their own essential Being has withdrawn and feel abandoned by it.

But what if, instead of fearing the pull of the ground, we draw into ourselves with our own being, follow it in its withdrawal from the all-dominating social Frame of existential calculation, success and failure. Such a *with-drawal* into ourselves may at first appear as an over-intense introversion and seriousness – an unwarranted or even pathological gravitas of being. Yet only through such a with-drawal do we come closer to the ground of our being – really 'go under'. This ground that we then meet is a supportive ground, giving us a buoyancy and confidence of step that is of a completely different order to the artificial cheerfulness, positivity and energetic vitality that are normally associated with health and well-being. This artificial buoyancy characterises the ideal 'lifestyles' presented by commercial advertising. The transparent 'little lie' of advertising is the way it attaches such lifestyles to the purchase and ownership of commodities. The far more serious lie of advertising – the 'big lie' is its role as a Goebbels-style propaganda medium for lifestyles in which people are so 'happy' or 'confident' in their ungroundedness that they no longer even feel the pull of the ground, feel the basic need and distress of a human being. In which "Beings strut as beings and yet are abandoned by Being." In contrast to this lie, Heidegger speaks of truth, a truth

"...grounded as the ground through that which we call *Da-sein*, as that which sustains man and is entrusted to him only rarely, as both donation and destiny, and only to those among men who are creative and are grounding....To be this *Da* is a destiny of man, in correspondence to which he grounds that which is itself the ground of the highest possibilities of his Being."

"The dislocation of man back into his ground has to be carried out in the first place by those few, solitary and uncanny ones, who in various ways as poets, thinkers, as builders and artists, as doers and actors, ground and shelter the truth of Being in beings through the transformation of beings."

To many the language of these paragraphs will appear not only obscure or opaque but even pathological or psychotic. Heidegger concurs:

"If we appraise the reflection on this dislocation of man from the standpoint of sound common sense and its predominance, we will reject it as deranged...and will not even take the pains to reject such a reflection but will simply ridicule it."

The addiction to common sense ways of speaking and writing, listening and thinking is threatened by what Bion called 'the mystic' and Heidegger refers to as 'uncanny ones'. Someone who is grounded is also grounding. Through their very presence we feel more intensely the pull of our own ground. And yet breaking the addiction to 'common sense' is as tortuous, slow and difficult a process as breaking an addiction to heroin. Many who try it 'break down' in the process – a fact which provides 'common sense' with a convenient excuse to ridicule and avoid what Heidegger calls 'decisive meditations'. It gives us good 'reason' to draw back from our own ground rather than allowing ourself to 'go under'. Common sense prescribes the 'keep your spirits **up**' mentality.

The spiritual tone of Heidegger's language is not the radiant lightness and joy of New Age 'spirituality'. The latter is an ungrounded spirituality, indeed a spirituality *of* ungroundedness – seeking the heights and the 'light' but fearing the depths and its unutterable tones. It seeks to promote a 'lightness of being' that is ultimately unsustainable and 'unbearable'. In psychoanalytic terms it corresponds to what is called the 'manic defence'. Such a spirituality is well-suited to application by business gurus in whipping up new frenzies of positive thinking to counter the fear of capitalist breakdown. The earth is the living symbol of the ground within each of us. The ridicule poured on 'friends of the earth' – those who respond to the call of the Earth and its need, who stop to think instead of pressing ahead with redoubled effort – is comparable to the ridicule that 'common sense' pours on psychoanalysis and on philosophy. This ridicule would seem even more justified to itself were reporters to have attended those privately arranged meetings (the so-called *Zollikoner* Seminars) in which the philosopher Heidegger and his friend, the psychiatrist Medard Boss engaged in dialogue with an informal circle of invited doctors and psychologists. The long silences which intervened in these dialogues and the way of listening they concealed are as incomprehensible to common sense as the 'Heideggerian' way of speaking which they facilitated – the language of Being.

A grounded thinking means a thinking grounded in listening. A grounded listening, a listening grounded in being, involves periods of patient silence which 'common sense' finds disturbing, threatening, crazy or ridiculous. That is why grounded listening where it exists, tends to be restricted and bounded by psychoanalytic or psychotherapeutic sessions – and why grounded listeners can make their careers only as patient shrinks or as mental patients.

The addiction to common sense is also reflected in an addiction to a psychological vocabulary of mental and emotional states that ignores their ontological dimension – their ground in Being. Philosophical counselling seeks not only a way of speaking or writing but a way of listening which hears beneath the vocabulary of the rational mind and of the emotions. The focus of such a way of listening is the inner bearing and posture of the speaker – their mental, emotional and bodily relation to what I have called the pull of the ground – to the core of their own being. An individual's thinking, feeling and willing can be more or less grounded and grounding – more or less responsive to the pull of the ground. A grounded inner bearing is created not by manipulating our physical, emotional or intellectual posture but by surrendering such manipulation to a process of inward listening. This process of inward listening is one in which we let our own centre of awareness go under and drop anchor, allowing it to sink downwards and inwards towards the depths of our being – finding support in a centre or core which is at the same time its true ground. This is a process that is automatically encouraged by the grounding listening of an external listener.

Many people find that when they are tired or even depressed, though they sparkle less they become better listeners. The withdrawal of the depressed, the disinclination to talk or be cheered up has as its flip side a heightened capacity to bear silence, and potentially – to listen to others. 'Depressive' discourse, despite its 'cynicism', 'pessimism' or 'gloominess', may also reveal a penetrating insight. This is an insight borne of silent and wordless knowing rather than verbal intellection. Depression, like aging and fatigue, is associated with a slowing down of our responses. This slowing down is seen negatively in a Western culture which associates intelligence with IQ – with quick thinking and fast reaction times. It has lost its sense of the 'wisdom of age', a wisdom in which it is precisely the absence of quick reactions that allows an authentic and more grounded inner response to gather from our depths.

It may at first seem fatuous to speak of depression in these positive terms. Is this not to ignore the negative emotions which characterise it – feelings of despair, hopelessness, unworthiness, shame, guilt, failure, weakness, inadequacy, entrapment, isolation, loss, envy, rage, helplessness etc.? The list can go on – in fact, it is doubtful if there is a single 'negative emotion' which has not been associated with depression or posited as its central feature by one 'psychology of depression' or another. This fact alone should give us pause to thought and question the meaning of 'depression'. Conversely, there is hardly a single positive emotion (joy, wonder, exultation, delight etc) that is not part of the experience of so-called 'mania'. So what then are depression, mania and 'manic depression'?

Were such a broad spectrum of emotional experience to be expressed through music or painting, we would marvel at the genius of the artist. Were all these emotions to form part of a counsellor's first-hand experience, it would enhance their range and depth of empathic understanding. What then, makes the difference between a great artist or counsellor and a person suffering from 'depression' or 'manic depression'? One difference is that both art and counselling emotion is transmuted into *feeling tone*. The artist does not express emotions but tones and colours of feeling. The counsellor transmutes emotions into wavelengths of attunement. Counsellors do not represent or describe their own emotional history or experience in speech but use feeling tone to attune their listening to others. The difference between feeling tones and emotions is that we do not attach labels to the former – any more than we do to colour tones or musical tones – whereas emotions are labelled by words and linked with verbal thinking and verbal judgements. Nowhere, I believe, is this better expressed than in the writings of Seth:

"Your emotional feelings are often transitory, but beneath there are certain qualities of feeling uniquely your own, that are like deep musical chords. While your day-to-day feelings may rise or fall, these characteristic feeling tones lie beneath. Sometimes they rise to the surface, but in great long rhythms. You cannot call these negative or positive. They are instead tones of your being. Once you learn to get the feeling of your own inner tone, then you are aware of its power, strength, and durability, and you can to some extent ride with it into deeper realities of experience. It is the essence of yourself. Its sweeps are broad in range, however. It does not determine, for example, specific events. It paints the colours in the large 'landscape' of your experience. It is the feeling of yourself, inexhaustible. In other terms it represents the expression of yourself in pure energy, from which your individuality rises, the You of you, unmistakeably given identity that is never duplicated. This energy comes from the core of BEING, from All That Is, and represents the source of never-ending vitality. It is Being, Being in You."

15. The Will to Meaning
— 'logotherapy' and 'cognitive' counselling

'Cognitive' and 'rational-emotive' approaches to counselling attribute negative emotions largely to the negative self-judgements that characterise the depressive person's spontaneous thoughts – judgements which reflect the individual's core beliefs or 'schemata'. These beliefs and the thoughts which express them function as self-fulfilling prophecies. They bring about situations which seem to confirm them, or evoke the very feelings they seem to 'express'. If I believe I am bad I feel bad. Feeling bad is then evidence that I 'am' bad. If I think I am boring to others I prevent myself from authentically relating to them, which leads them to avoid me and confirms that I am boring for them.

The understanding that cognitive psychology gives us of the role of thoughts and beliefs in emotional life is a crucial and a necessary one, and yet it is, I believe insufficient as a basis for therapeutic practice. The counsellor may help the client to understand the role of their own thoughts, attitudes and beliefs in shaping their emotional life, and help them to alter these beliefs as necessary. Such counselling provides, then, a form of 'empowering' education for the client – teaching the latter to take responsibility for their own well-being.

This is not the whole story, however. Counsellors, analysts, and therapists, as we know, are not themselves immune from depression or other forms of mental suffering, despite their developed awareness. What *distinguishes* the counsellor from the 'ill' client therefore is not awareness or training alone. It is the fact that the counsellor is not exclusively concerned with his or her own well-being but with the well-being of others, does not just take responsibility for themselves but is 'response-able' to others. Similarly, the artist cares not just for their own well-being but for their work, and what it communicates to others. The negative experience of the 'ill' is implicitly also a *negative capability* and negative *response-ability* – capable of adding value to their lives and relationships to exactly the same degree that it now seems to denude their lives of value. But this negative capability cannot be fulfilled except through a positive response-ability to something beyond themselves and their own well-being, through a focus of consciousness and intent that is precisely not on their emotional 'problems', however these are experienced or stated.

Paradoxically therefore, it is precisely by virtue of their counselling role – one which puts the focus of the counselling relationship on the client rather than the counsellor – that counselling tends to reinforce the client's focus on themselves rather than on something or someone beyond themselves. This focus is not in itself 'unhealthy' – though it may already have become so by the time someone comes for counselling. It is however, one-sided. For through the counselling or analytic relationship the counsellor or analyst is enabled to perceive directly or indirectly every aspect of the client's being and relating except the most crucial one – the client's *own* capacity to listen and respond in a caring way to someone else. For that someone else is in the case the counsellor or analyst, who is not there to be 'counselled' or 'analysed'. This is the paradoxical limit or boundary of all approaches to counselling. The question is whether this paradoxical boundary is ignored or acknowledged as a defining boundary. If the latter, then this boundary is automatically transcended as a boundary. So far as I am aware there are only two approaches to counselling or therapy which implicitly address this question. One is 'logotherapy', the approach to counselling and therapy created by the concentration camp survivor Viktor Frankl. Frankl distinguished between the will for health, success, money, happiness or self-actualisation with what he called 'the will to meaning.' This he links with 'self-transcendence':

"Self-transcendence is the essence of existence.....Man's struggle for his self and his identity is doomed to failure unless it is enacted as dedication and devotion to something beyond his self, to something above his self."

The other approach is 'communicative psychoanalysis' (Langs) , which was founded on the recognition that patients in analysis invariably say or do things which, on one level seem to be intended to *help* the analyst. The analysand analyses the analyst in other words, as well as the other way round. This is not a mere hypothesis but an expression of the very nature of meaning. Meaning (noun) derives not just from experience, sensations or perceptions, from feeling, words or symbols but from meaning (verb). From meaning someone or something beyond oneself – intending an Other (the analysand *intending* the analyst for example). In this sense Frankl's 'will to meaning' is itself synonymous with 'self-transcendence', for it is the will (intent) to mean (intend) an Other.

Philosophical counselling is based explicitly on the recognition that all personal questions reveal trans-personal or 'philosophical' ones, that human emotions are not essentially private property but wavelengths of attunement to other beings, that the meaning of meaning (noun) is also meaning (verb), and that along with this goes the recognition that the opportunity to talk about and 'hear' ourselves that counselling provides is insufficient – that true health and well-being require the deepening and fulfilment of a client's capacity to *listen* to others whilst staying in touch with themselves. To *be* with others in a *meaningful* way.

There are clients who find it easy to focus on others but find it difficult to attend to their own feelings and own needs. They do not recognise that an authentic relatedness to others is impossible without fully being ourselves and inseparable from a deep self-awareness. Conversely there are those who focus obsessively on themselves and do not recognise that self-awareness and self-fulfilment require, paradoxically, a focus transcending the self. Listening always has a dual inward and outward focus. We cannot listen to others unless we are also capable of listening inwardly to ourselves. Philosophical counselling takes listening as *paradigmatic* for a focus of consciousness that is both self-aware and other-oriented. A way of being oneself and fulfilling one's own potential for being through one's being with others and being for others.

Meditational practices are essentially self-oriented. Counselling is essentially other-oriented. Listening is a meditative activity that is other-oriented. Philosophical counselling is meditative listening.

Cognitive counselling has also been seen as a form of philosophical counselling originating with the Stoics. In 'Counselling for Depression' Gilbert writes:

"These philosophers were concerned with the nature of subjective meaning – what is beauty, what is honour, what is justice? None of these questions can be answered by recourse to objective science, but rather arise from the application of various (often personal) criteria. Consequently, the Stoics were interested in the qualities that make up subjective meaning, and they developed a method of inquiry to do this, called the Socratic Method of Dialogue. This dialogue was designed to reveal the underlying criteria for meaning....and to explore the process of reasoning by which an individual comes to a certain view."

Gilbert sees the cognitive counsellor as engaging the client in a form of Socratic dialogue. This does not mean debating, arguing, advising or persuading. Nor is it "positive thinking, looking on the bright side or ignoring negative or social realities" but rather "exploring personal meaning and attempting to change states of mind by a gentle revelation that labels like inferiority are subjective judgements not facts."

By 'labels such as inferiority' Gilbert refers implicitly to the client's *language* – the beliefs and attitudes this embodies, the spontaneous thoughts or inner speech that these generate, and the emotions which they both label and evoke. It is the clients mental vocabulary and phraseology, in other words their language, that shapes both their thoughts and their feelings.

Gilbert refers to the client's 'automatic' or 'pop-up' thoughts as those "not arrived at through reflective reasoning." On the other hand he declares that "their most salient aspect is their core of meaning.". It is not through question and answer type of 'Socratic' dialogue that we become aware of our automatic thoughts however, but through a listening attention to the language in which we couch our statements and question. And it is not through reflective reasoning alone that we approach a 'core of meaning' but through a listening which quests the essential truth of language, those pre-verbal and pre-linguistic dimensions of being which underlie both our thoughts and our emotions.

Philosophical Counselling understands the inter-relation of thoughts as the expression of a more fundamental inter-relation of language and being, the Frame and the Ground. Our choice of language shapes both our intellectual and emotional life. At the same time it can conceal a 'core of meaning' that has to do with essential dimensions of being. The dimensions of being are essentially inter-personal and trans-personal, for they have to do with fundamental values and with questions of being both of which transcend the individual. That does not mean they are not also highly individual. For whilst each of us has a unique set of values, any given value – like any given gene – is something that we share in common with others and also embody in our own unique way. Values are essentially nameless. They communicate through but not in a client's words. They are more than just unspoken words, thoughts or feelings, but the client's essential language of being. They are what the client embodies for the counsellor and donates to the counselling relationship – just as an atom donates electrons to a molecular bond. The value (electron) then becomes a shared value. The counsellor needs a certain 'affinity' or 'valency' (an electron 'hole') to be silently receptive to this donation and to recognise the values that the client embodies as a gift that the client brings to be received and shared. This is how we inwardly **heed** the client's message to us as individuals, showing a respectful receptivity to the inner being and inner knowing that dwells beneath their surface language and emotional suffering.

In summary, therefore, the 'method' of philosophical counselling consists in:

(1) listening to the personal *language* in which the client articulates their thoughts and feelings.

(2) helping to articulate the common questions of *being* which underlie and transcend this language.

(3) being receptive to the client's unique *language of being* – their essential values and way of being.

(4) embodying and thereby modelling a way of *listening* that allows one to attend to others whilst staying with oneself and communicating from one's very being.

For the individual 'being' means not only being oneself but being with others. Socially, it means learning to be oneself with others. This means finding a way of being oneself in which one can also be comfortable with and accept others. It also means finding a way of being with others in which one is comfortable with and accepting of oneself. Learning to relate is not just about doing or being done to, it is therefore also about being. Finding a way of relating to or even counselling another person means finding a way of being with that person. And finding a *way of being with another* often involves finding *another way of being*. To begin with this means appreciating the other's way of being – not just as their way of being – as private property – but as a way of value to us, a way we too can follow. This does not mean mimicking another person's words or deeds, but following them along their of way of being – even whilst leading them upon ours. This is like listening to and learning a foreign language – learning another language of being in order to respond and communicate from our own being.

16. Being and Relating — a generic case study

"Meaning can be in the world because it is in being." (Buber)

We do not 'have' relationships – we are relational beings. Again, we do not need to place psychological 'projections' upon people or to internalise them as psychological 'introjects' in order for them to mean something to us – in order for their whole way of being to speak to us in some way and recall us to an aspect of our own being.

"It is a different matter when in a receptive hour of my personal life a man meets me about whom there is something which I cannot grasp in any objective way at all, that 'says something to me'. That does not mean, says to me what manner of man this is, what is going on in him, and the like. But it means, says something to me, addresses something to me, speaks something that enters my own life." (Martin Buber)

Each of us not only speaks a language. Each of us is a language. The language that we are is our 'language of being' – our way of being and the qualities and values this embodies. Relational problems have a lot to do with the way in which we name and interpret such essential qualities of being in words – for it is this that shapes our emotional responses. To get beneath the tangles of our verbal and emotional responses means not taking each other's words and deeds 'literally' but seeing them as translations of essential qualities of being. In order to sense these qualities in the first place we must be able to identify with them. In this way they recall us to aspects or potentials of our own being and thereby extend our own 'language of being.'

Readers of this essay might find it unusual that a work dealing with an approach to counselling includes no case studies. This is because, by definition, no written case study can bring out the wordless comprehensions and inner responses that belong to the essence of 'being and listening'. What follows is a not an actual individual case study therefore, but rather a 'generic' case study.

It's aim is to use a fictional example to show how verbal constructs in general interfere with a listening that is rooted in being and oriented to individual 'languages of being'. The case study is generic in another sense also. Philosophical counselling makes no distinction in principle between the theoretical constructs placed by counsellors upon relationships – whether in relationship counselling or the counselling relationship itself – and the personal constructs placed upon a relationship by either counsellor or client. Both types of construct create a listening perspective framed and limited by language and divorced from being.

Bill and Laura 'have' a relationship. They also have a problem 'in' this relationship. Bill reacts with anger to Laura's 'untidiness'. Laura regards Bill's fastidiousness as 'neurotic' and 'obsessional'. Their differences are a constant source of hostility, resentment and conflict. Relationship challenges such as this can be seen in a number of different ways. It might be said, for example, that Bill's fastidiousness is indeed a form of 'compulsive neurosis', a product of his childhood upbringing. His behaviour might be seen as resulting from the 'introjection' of a parental figure. Something similar might be said of Laura's untidiness. Alternatively it may speculated that Bill's hostility is really a hostility to a 'part' of himself, an 'internal object' projected 'on' or 'into' Laura. A philosophical understanding requires none of these 'psychological' constructs. It starts from the simple fact that Bill sees Laura as being 'sluttish' and Laura sees Bill as being 'neurotic'. In doing so both are in effect identifying each other's *being* with something that can be labelled in words. The degree to which their words accurately describe each other's behaviour is not of principal importance here, but the fact that they each conflate their partner's essential language of being with its behavioural translation.

Laura's way of being is a language with its own aesthetic. This aesthetic is different to that of Bill. Bill senses and appreciates this aesthetic but however has no words to express it. Laura, however has already translated her own aesthetic not into words but into deeds — into behaviour. Her untidiness is an attempt to be herself – to translate her own relaxed music into a style of behaviour. Bill, likewise, translates his own language of being – his own more structured and austere music – into the fastidiousness that is the mark of his character. Whilst neither Bill nor Laura have words for each other's essential language of being, they do have words for each other's behaviour. Bill labels Laura as 'messy' and Laura labels Bill as 'neurotic'. These verbal interpretations of each other are understandable. Bill has not 'projected' something on Laura – she herself has translated aspects of her own essential way of being into a behavioural language characterised by untidiness. Laura does not need to 'project' neuroticism onto Bill. He himself has translated his own language of being into something that fits the verbal description of 'compulsive behaviour'.

There is a 'common sense' approach to relational problems such as these which suggests that the individuals involved should negotiate a realistic compromise, one that goes some way towards meeting each other's needs on the issue that divides them – in this case the question of 'tidiness'. This approach concentrates on outward behaviour only, ignoring the deeper issues of what unites people in a relationship – of what they mean to one another. Laura and Bill mean something to one another by virtue of who they are – their languages of being. Both embody for the other a different aesthetic – a different language of being. Were Bill not only to appreciate but to identify with Laura's aesthetic this would transform his own language of being and its expression in behaviour. For he could then embody his aesthetic of 'care-fullness' in her more 'care-free' way and vice versa. If Laura were not only to sense but to identify with Bill's aesthetic her own language of being would alter and so would its behavioural translation. Identification with someone is not the same as verbal identification of some aspect of their being – identifying them as being 'this'.

Identifying with someone means not just finding a common language on the level of words or behaviour but to find a common language of being – a common music. Even just to like someone is in a sense to liken yourself to them – to acknowledge a common wavelength of being that unites you with the other person – and that therefore is as much a 'part' of you as it is of 'them'. For Bill to 'liken' himself to Laura does not imply that he should like or imitate Laura's untidy behaviour. For Laura to liken herself to Bill does not imply that she should become compulsively orderly like Bill. But nor is it simply a question of them meeting somewhere halfway. For Bill and Laura to liken themselves to each other does not mean that they should like each other's behaviour but seek to appreciate the underlying aesthetic that this behaviour translates – or mis-translates.

By opening himself to Laura's fundamental aesthetic Bill could begin to perceive underneath her behaviour a value transcending 'untidiness' – the possibility of a carefree and spontaneous orderliness as opposed to his own controlled and controlling sense of order. Conversely, Laura could perceive beneath Bill's 'neuroticism' a value beyond the words 'neurotic', or 'compulsive'- a carefulness that relaxes – which frees one of cares and facilitates the 'care-freeness' that is her chief value.

If 'I am I' and 'you are you' and we are both merely self-contained identities, then it does not matter how 'OK' I am for you and vice versa. Relating is no more about mere 'OK-ness' or 'acceptance' than it is about conflict. Relating is not a matter of remaining the same or becoming different, protecting our identity or changing it, but is about broadening our language of being to embrace new values. Values are not private property – they are the very bonds that unite individuals in relationships.

They are difficult to describe in words because they do not have to do with similarities or differences but with sameness-in-difference and difference-in-sameness – the hidden bonds which make individuals alike in the very ways in which they seem to each other to be different, and vice versa. They are potentialities of being that each individual combines and expresses in their own way.

If two individuals were totally identical they would have no relationship – for they would constitute one being and not two. If two individuals were totally different they would likewise have no relationship – for there would be no common ground between them. This does not mean however, that any two individuals are alike 'in certain respects' and different 'in other respects'. For were this to be the case they would also have no relationship whatsoever. Their differences being pure differences there would be no common ground. Their similarities being pure similarities they would carry no trace of distinctness or otherness. That is why individuals always express the 'same' values differently or express different values in similar ways. They are comparable to the resemblances to ourselves that we see when we look at a photograph of relatives – they cannot be pinned down by saying that two people have the 'same' nose, or the same eyes – for no two noses or pairs of eyes are ever identical. Just as two people may share common genes even though they have no biological relationship, so they may share common values even though they are unrelated biologically or culturally. It is because of this that values – and not biology, ethnicity or verbally codified moralities – are the basis of lasting relationships.

Bill and Laura have the capacity to 'love' each other – to value each other's language of being. But they confuse identifying with each other's values with something quite different – with tolerating, accepting or taking on the expression of these values in words and behaviour. We do not 'have' values – they are the common alphabet of being from whose words we are. They shape us, as our genes do. Each in-dividual is an in-divisible and unique combination of certain values. And yet these values are also what unites them, like common genes, with other individuals. In relationship counselling it is above all important to distinguish philosophically between being and language, languages of being and their translation in word and deed, between the values that unite people in relationships and the outward attitudes and stances that divide them.

Helping relationships to survive and deepen means helping individuals to acknowledge what they mean to one another – their sameness-in-difference. This means (a) seeing beneath a partner's words and behaviour to something that is of value to oneself and (b) learning to identify with and embody this value in everyday life, albeit in one's own way. Such a philosophical approach to relationship counselling may seem far removed from the daily grind of sexual, marital and extra-marital conflicts that confronts the relationship counsellor. Whether it is or is not depends on the counsellor's capacity to perceive values and 'languages of being' as well as emotional and relational behaviours or 'patterns'. To understand a couple's problems means here again, to 'stand under' the language with which it presents itself – both verbal, emotional and behavioural. And yet for a counsellor to counsel clients about their relationships is not possible if they do not themselves relate to the client. The word 'relate' means to carry or bear back (*latus* – borne). To relate means to receive someone in their being, allowing the very aspects of their being which strike us as foreign or different to address us in our being and in doing so to recall us to an aspect or potential of our own being. This is the 'value' of their words – not what they are about nor what they 'express'. This is also what adds value to our own verbal response – ensuring that through it we bear something back to the other from our own being as well as in words – that we relate.

17. The Borderline of Psychology — language and psychosis

Since Freud, interest in psychology has grown enormously. Much 'psycho-babble' ('the unconscious', 'repressed feelings', 'positive mental attitude' etc) has entered ordinary vocabulary. An ever-growing number of different psychological approaches to counselling and therapy, each with their own professional terminologies, compete with one another in the 'psycho-market'.

Psychologising is a way of speaking that reduces all human problems, questions and suffering to 'feelings' i.e. 'unresolved', 'threatening' or 'repressed' emotions and emotional conflicts. This apparent validation and affirmation of the significance of feeling and emotional life is in fact its opposite. For the therapeutic 'working through' or 'resolution' of repressed or unresolved feelings, emotional conflicts etc. always turns out to have something to do with representing them verbally – whether or not such verbal representation is preceded by a phase of non-verbal experiencing or expression (catharsis). The function of verbal representation however, is precisely to facilitate a dis-identification with our emotions.

When someone says 'I feel tired' or 'I feel a lot of anger towards my father', the subject, verb and object are insulated from one another. The linguistic subject – the 'I' or 'ego' – is not this 'tiredness' or 'anger'. As egos we 'have' feelings. Though they cannot but affect our sense of who we are, the word 'I' allows us to simultaneously acknowledge a feeling and to dis-identify from it.

The understanding of so-called 'borderline' and 'psychotic states' is impossible from such an ego-psycho-logical standpoint. For in such states an assertion of the form 'I am tired' may imply not just that 'I have a feeling of tiredness' but that 'I **am** my tiredness.' Not just that 'I feel bad' but that 'I **am** bad'. There is no longer an 'I' that is distinct from its own experiencing. There is no sense that even though I 'have' certain feelings I **am not** these feelings. Instead it is the 'I' itself that is not. To ask someone in such a state 'How are you?' or 'How are you feeling?' is to beg the question and can reinforce the individual's sense of verbal incapacity, of wordlessness and worthlessness.

The writings of Samuel Beckett are unique in addressing and expressing the paradox of an 'I' that no longer has reality to itself. In 'The Unnameable' he writes:

"I, say I. Unbelieving.....I seem to speak, it is not I, about me, it is not about me. Nothing. These few general remarks to begin with."

The borderline to psychosis is the borderline of 'psychological' language and theory itself. It is the borderline between what or how we feel and who we feel ourselves to be. It is the borderline of self and experience, language and being. On one side of this border is language and the linguistic ego or 'I'. Here, subject and predicate, the self's experience and its experience of itself, are linguistically distinct and separable. On the other side of this border is the reality that self and experience, what we feel and who we are, though distinct, cannot ultimately be separated. They are distinct but inseparable aspects of our being.

Who we are cannot be separated from what we think or feel, have or do. We are what we think, feel, have and do – and yet we are also always more than what we feel or experience within any given moment. The illusion that there is an 'I' which is not merely *distinct* but *separable* from my experience is an illusion of the language mind. This illusion is the basis of normal ego-identity and ego-functioning. In psychosis this separation breaks down to such an extent that ego-identity is not merely *in*-separable from its experience but also in-*distinct* from it. I **am** tiredness, badness, confusion etc.

Illness of any sort affects ego-identity to some degree. With headache, cold or fever I feel 'out of sorts'. I sense that I am not quite myself. The 'I' that has this headache, cold or fever is not quite the same 'I' as the one I usually know. My experience of this illness affects my sense of the self that is experiencing it. But I keep my head above water somehow – I retain a sense that I am more than what I am experiencing right now. That allows me to say 'I have a cold' rather than feel that 'I am this cold'.

Illness of any sort becomes chronic when the individual identifies with it and loses any sense of being more than how they currently experience themselves to be. The answer that both medicine and psychology implicitly offer is always to re-establish an illusory separation of identity and being, self and experience. Medicine encourages the patient to think of the illness as an object, as something that he or she has. Psychologising encourages patients to think of feelings and relationships as something that they have. Both medicine and psychology seek the cause and remedy of suffering in terms of what they 'have done' or 'can do', or in terms of what has been or can be done. They cater for the ego.

Philosophical Counselling is a way of relating and responding to others based not on psychology but on 'ontology'. Ontology is a philosophical term deriving from the Greek words 'ontos' and 'logos'. Ontos means being. Logos means word, speech or language. The language of Philosophical Counselling is the language of 'being'.

Heidegger noted that the verb 'to be' is unlike all others. It is a primal verb or proto-verb in the sense that it always implies other verbs. 'I **am** a father' implies I *have* children. 'I am hungry' implies I *need* something to *eat*. 'I **am** tired' can imply many things – that 'I feel tired', 'I want to go to bed', 'I've had enough television', 'Can you go now?', 'This seminar has gone on too long' etc.

Of course, statements without the verb 'to be' can also carry multiple meanings. 'I feel tired' can also mean 'I want to go to bed' or 'I want to be alone'. In a therapeutic or analytic context 'I have a lot of anger towards my father' can mean 'I feel a lot of anger towards you – my therapist', or even 'You are harbouring anger towards me, seeing me as your father.'

Transference is in this sense a type of displacement of the personal pronoun. The analyst acknowledges such transference by recognising that an 'it', 'he' or 'she' may displace a 'you', or vice versa. The analytic interpretation of transference is in this sense a type of verbal translation. The belief is not only that people can say one thing but mean another, but that both meanings are verbally representable. Heidegger on the other hand, saw the quest for philosophical truth as a type of 'essential translation' or 'inner-lingual translation'. This is not the translation of one language or one word into another. Nor is it the expression of pre-verbal feelings or experience in ordinary words. Essential translation returns language to the primacy of being and returns us to the word being – a word that is the emptiest, least saturated of words and yet paradoxically the fullest.

For just as the verb to be always implies another, more concrete verb, so conversely do concrete verbs always imply something to do with our being. Anything we say in words is an expression of our being and a translation of our own 'language of being'. Essential translation *returns* the word as verb to its origin in being and to our own language of being. It does so by using a language which has at its centre the actual word being and the verb to be. For unlike others, it belongs to the essence of these empty words that they can be used to hint at and communicate meanings that otherwise elude language – that cannot be defined 'in other words' or with other verbs.

The difference between interpretation and essential translation, is expressed in the contrast between psychological and ontological discourse. There is an essential difference, for example between a psychological discourse that deals with the nature of human relating and relationships, and an ontological discourse that translates the essence of relating as 'being with' (*Mitsein*). There is an essential difference between a discourse which sees listening as a skill and one which understands it as an activity of being and a way of being with. There is an essential difference between an understanding of discourse and language themselves in terms of linguistics or psychoanalysis and Heidegger's understanding of language as the 'house of being'.

The difference between psychological and ontological discourse, however, is not merely a question of language or terminology, of 'psycho-babble' or 'Freud-speak' for example, versus 'Heideggerese'. What Heidegger calls 'essential translation' is not only a way of speaking but a way of listening. This is a way of listening pointed to by Bion when he wrote of the state of mind necessary to understand psychotic speech. This is a state of mind that is freed of 'sensuous' associations, memories and desires and therefore open to perceiving the 'non-sensuous reality' of the psyche. This is not merely a reference to unconscious communication but to what a person's words tell us about their relationship to language and to the linguistic 'I' or 'ego' – their way of *being in the word*. Bion intuitively understood that a psychotic way of 'being in the word' is quite different from a normal or 'neurotic' use of language. He constantly sought to distinguish between the ordinary meaning or use of a word or phrase and its meaning and use in psychotic states.

Psychotic states cannot be interpreted in saturated words, images, symbols and concepts – however much they describe intense or primal emotions. Like religious words and images, most emotional vocabularies and psychoanalytic concepts have long since become saturated or over-saturated by meanings accruing from past experience. The word being, unlike the word God, is a word that forever escapes such saturation. Both psychologist and psychotics however attempt to use saturated concepts or sensuous language to translate and communicate their own reality. To hear behind and beyond this language requires a type of listening that goes together with essential translation.

It is not negative feelings of anxiety, fear, guilt, anger, worthlessness, pain, shame (or of joy, love, enthusiasm, delight etc) that produce suffering, depression or mania. Nor is it the repression of these feelings. It is the way we identify with or dis-identify from these feelings. To repress or express is an act of the ego, something someone does. To identify with something or someone is not an ordinary act – something that 'I' do. For by definition, the act of identification *with* something or someone alters the identity of the agent. Such acts are not acts of doing but *acts of being*. 'To be' is the proto-verb because beneath all acts of doing is our inner *activity of being*.

'To be or not to be?' In psychotic states the 'I' is not. It is what it feels and nothing more. Being is identified and merged with one dimension, one potential or aspect of itself. Therefore the 'I' is not anything distinct from or apart from this one potential for being, this one self, this one desire, feeling or thought. As a result, whatever the specific nature of this feeling is, whether anger or joy, fullness or emptiness, delight or despair, it separates the 'I' from being-as-a-whole. Because the 'I' is not, because it is what it feels, it does not feel that it fully **is**. Loss of ego is tantamount to non-being. The 'I' cannot therefore say accurately or literally what, when, where or how 'I am'. It is not this 'I'. Instead it may be an 'it', 'he', 'she' or 'you'. Thoughts tell the 'I' that it is bad, it is dying, it is guilty or worthless not because it 'has' these feelings but because it has nothing else – because these negative feelings and the negative words which name them are an endless attempt to give the 'I' a positive determination – to allow it to be rather than not be. The essential message of ontology to psychiatry, analysis and therapy is the same as the call of the 'psychotic', essentially translated. This is the call and desire to be.

'If I am alone and seemingly unreachable, it is because I do not know how to be with people and because they do not know how to be with me. It is not that I do not want to be with anybody or that nobody wants to be with me – to talk or to help – but nobody wants or is able to *be* with me. You wonder how the voices of my persecutory thoughts can be stilled or silenced? They are 'not-I' because my 'I' is not. Shall 'I' describe them to you. How will this help me to be? In wishing me to describe my 'feelings', to say how 'I' feel, and what 'I' experience, you wish me to split my 'I' from my feelings and my experience and therefore from my being. This has failed for me in the past, else why would 'I' be ill. I see that it does not work that perfectly for you either. You say 'I want to help you'. I do not hear your 'I'. I hear you better than the 'I' you offer me. I respond to you, not this 'I'. That is why I do not speak or speak in a way that is crazy to you. I hear you. You do not hear me because you cannot tolerate being without an 'I'. I cannot tolerate it either – that is why I am in pain. You want me to 'share' my pain, you want to 'empathise' with me but you do not really want to feel it – you know it would overwhelm your 'I'. You feel that you are. I do not feel that I am. I am only what I feel. You like people to talk about their 'feelings'. You 'have' feelings. But do you want to know these feelings – to feel them? You are not your feelings. I am what I feel. Do not tell me what I am – that I am 'ill', that I am 'angry', that I am 'envious'. Help me feel by the way you listen that I am *not* my feelings and not my thoughts, not my behaviour and not my words, not these voices and not my body. Do not respond to 'me' as 'I' am. Do not be considerate and 'receptive' or clinical and 'objective'. Do not see how I am and help me with it. Know that I am not this . Communicate this 'knowing' and not your 'knowledge' or 'sensitivity'. Be *more* than a doctor, psychiatrist, friend, counsellor or therapist, more than your role, knowledge and insight. In this way you will help me to feel that I am more than what I feel myself to be now. You may feel impotent in knowing what to do or say to me, how to 'relate' to me. That is all right. What I want is for you to simply be with me, if you can. Help me to be more of who I am by being more of who you are with me. Grant time to fully *be* with me in silence. Then maybe I will slowly feel safe in being more of who I am with you. Did nobody teach you how to be with someone in silence, how to restrain your questions, your polite nods and positive encouragements, your immaculate mirroring words that tell me nothing that I do not already know, communicate nothing that comes from the core of your being and leave me isolated and alone? And did nobody teach you how, knowingly or unknowingly I sometimes drop an apparently meaningless or empty word in order to give you a clue – not in order for you to probe me about it or ignore it, but in order that you take it with you, spend time with it and grow into its seemingly empty spaces. For maybe then it will speak to you and tell you where I am.'

18. I and Thou
— separation, merger and authentic contact

We cannot be with someone without doing unless we are able to be with ourselves without doing. 'First being, then doing and being done to.' To be with someone does not require any doing however. It requires only that we lean or list towards them with our whole being – that we list-en. This is the only type of listening appropriate to people in psychotic or borderlines states. According to Hedges, the 'listening perspective' of the analyst does indeed need to change for the 'borderline' patient – in his terms to acknowledge the latter's need for 'merger' or 'symbiosis'.

"To the therapist symbiosis may be a theoretical construct, but to the borderline patient psychological merger is the only known form of emotional existence."

The partial truth in this statement is that insofar as the borderline patient experiences psychotic states he or she is merged with an aspect of their own being. As a result, they can be understood and relieved of the intensity of this identification only through some form of merger in which it is shared and partially contained by the therapist. Merger is the only alternative the borderline patient knows to ordinary neurotic and schizoid *separation* from their own being. The neurotic response to existential and emotional insecurity is a dis-identification from feelings achieved through language and the linguistic ego. The psychotic response is total identification with a partial aspect of our being.

The neurotic is governed by *merger anxiety*. Intimacy and merger experience are warded off or allowed only in controlled doses or in a managed role (therapist for example). A paranoid-schizoid strategy of compulsive dis-identification and diminution of their own feelings is utilised to avoid over-identification with any one aspect of their own being or the feelings of others. This is ultimately counter-productive, leading bit by bit to the accumulation of feelings of such overpowering intensity that they can no longer be managed by normal dis-identification and require active repression. The neurotic alternates between controlled placidity and catharsis – the latter preferably experienced vicariously, through films, novels or the emotional expression of others.

The psychotic on the other hand is governed by *separation anxiety*, fearful that any degree of dis-identification from any feeling or aspect of their being is tantamount to separation from their being-as-a-whole. This strategy is also counter-productive and paradoxical – for in identifying and clinging onto particular emotional states, they implicitly dis-identify with other potentials for being and therefore also cut themselves off from their being-as-a-whole. This can lead to a splitting and alternation of moods and 'sub-personalities'.

The neurotic seeks *ego-identity* divorced from being through reason and language, doing and having, but ends up merged with another, with an ideology or with the mass culture. The psychotic fears ego-identity and seeks *being* through merger and identification but ends up separate, alone and still threatened by non-being.

The neurotic seeks to avoid the ontological insecurity of the psychotic by achieving social, emotional and intellectual security but never succeeds quite fully. The psychotic faces constant ontological in-security and never achieves the 'ordinary unhappiness' of the neurotic. Neurosis and psychosis, separation and merger are the twin poles within which both psychic reality and psychological theory operate – distinct but inseparable. Dialectically related. Both constitute a mis-relation to being. Freudian psychoanalysis is a psychology of the neuroses. Melanie Klein went further and realised the inseparability of neurotic and psychotic dimensions of experience. But there can be no psychology of the borderline state without challenging the very dichotomy of separation and merger, neurosis and psychosis. This dichotomy is reflected in the simultaneous separation and merger of psychology and philosophy, emotional and ontological questions, that is often found in psychoanalytic literature. The less questions are addressed in explicitly philosophical terms, the more implicitly philosophical this literature becomes.

Between merger and separation is *contact*. Real inner contact between people does not abolish their distinctness and replace separation with merger. Many fear it will do so, seeking to replace contact with either separation or merger. In the analytic literature, however, contact is also confused with merger. Thus Hedges writes:

"I-Thou statements usually represent breaches of empathic contact, whereas 'we', 'us', and 'togetherness' statements resonate with the merger experience."

Not only does Hedges conflate empathic contact with merger, he also *merges* a psychological language with a philosophical one in a way that abolishes their distinctness. It was Martin Buber who used the term 'I-Thou relation' to indicate a way of being with others based on authentic contact. A contact and communication of being. Hedges identifies this intentional and wordless orientation of our own being towards the being of another with verbal statements of the 'I-You' form (e.g. '**I** feel hurt by **you**.'). This misses the very essence of the 'I-Thou' relation as Buber understood it. 'I-You' statements may well constitute 'breaches' of 'empathic contact', not because they reflect a genuine I-Thou relation but because they translate this trans-personal relation of being into a purely personal or inter-personal relation.

Words such as 'I feel discomforted by you' or even 'I feel discomforted by our relationship' are an objectification of the between, of the relationship as 'cause' of my feelings, and of those feelings themselves. The feelings become private property – my 'hurt' rather than a feeling between us that we share. Hedges is aware of this when he writes, of a particular 'borderline' patient that:

"When the therapist shifted [from 'I-you' statements] to the 'we have something troublesome which somehow together we must solve', the patient's distress subsided."

The therapist's shifting to a 'we' mode of discourse is presented as if it itself were merely a linguistic shift rather than a fundamental shift in the therapist's orientation of being – towards awareness and affirmation of the 'between'. The point is not simply for the therapist to speak about this between using words like 'we' or 'us' – they could just as well speak about 'the relationship'. The point is to speak to the other from the site of authentic contact – *from* the between.

This 'between' as Buber described it can be compared to the 'potential space' which Winnicott spoke of. It is the meeting ground itself – the 'place' where people really meet and make contact with one another. In the contact of human beings who are really *with* each other, the separation of one being and another breaks down. Not because they merge empathically or adopt a new form of 'we' discourse, but because this contact is a contact of being. Where human beings are in authentic contact with one another, the boundary that distinguishes them is the very boundary that unites them. The 'Being of beings' in Heidegger's sense is an invisible point of contact between beings. For this contact point or surface is nothing in itself and yet it is everything. It unites beings as one and distinguishes each as unique.

Again – to listen is to list or lean with our whole being towards the being of another. To really *be* there with another, to extend a tendril of intent and establish contact with another human being that has nothing to do with what is spoken *about*. The speaking self says 'I' and 'you'. The listening self does not merely say 'we'. It hearkens wordlessly to the between, avoiding labels but touching, holding and handling the other in this between. The words of the listening self do not describe or interpret the between. They serve this between and sing its song. They do not describe or represent an 'unconscious communication'. They are part of it. For they are not 'about' relationships but acts of relating – inner gestures of **holding** and **handling**.

The activity of identification and dis-identification that underlies separation and merger states is a primal activity of being that occurs on either side of the contact boundary between two people. It is reflected in the processes that Melanie Klein calls 'splitting' and 'projective identification'. The translation of our primal activity of (dis-)identification into language results in verbal splitting – polarities such as 'good' vs 'bad'. What I identify with is identified *as* good. What I dis-identify from is identified *as* bad. The subject/object structure allows the bad to become a 'you' or 'it', and the good an 'I'. Such thinking identifies something as something else. In essence it identifies aspects of being and values with words and their meanings. In saying 'this is good', or 'that is bad', 'this is I' or 'that is you', it says in essence 'being is language'. Much of what we ordinarily call thinking, in other words, is governed by a fundamental mis-relation of language and being, dominated by the activity of (dis-)identification.

Beneath this level of thinking however, is another, more essential consciousness of self based not on identification or dis-identification but on *being-in-touch* – on contact and the contact boundary. To be in touch with oneself is to be aware of feelings and yet be aware that one is also more than these feelings. Our consciousness of self does not either identify or dis-identify with feelings or states of being of any sort but is the very boundary or border between one 'primary' or 'foreground' state of being and another, 'secondary' or 'background' one. Our consciousness may be focussed on one side of the border – our primary state of being – but this does not mean that we identify with it or lose touch with other states, aspects or dimensions of our being. It cannot, for it is the boundary itself, and as such in touch with both states. Only if our consciousness of self identifies with one of these states (psychotic action) does the other appear as a threat from the 'other side'. Only if our consciousness of self dis-identifies with its states of being (neurotic action) do they appear as detached and separate states – as 'internal objects' in need of 'integration'.

Every external relation or boundary of self and other is at the same time an internal relation or boundary between primary and secondary 'self-states'. Between a shared value or potential of the other's being that is primarily embodied by the self (primary self-state) and a potential of one's being that is primarily embodied by the other (secondary self-state or 'other self'). Relating to others always goes hand in hand with this spontaneous differentiation of self-states. We can respond to this differentiation by objectification, separation and polarisation of self-states – by 'splitting' and 'projective identification' – or by a consciousness of self which is in touch with both states, because it is sited at their boundary. The latter generates a type of thinking in which we become simultaneously and spontaneously aware of two or more sides of ourselves, two or more distinct aspects of the same issue, two or more distinct feelings or meanings – but without separating them. We do not treat them as separate 'things' – as external or internal objects. We do not equate them or oppose them to one another conceptually. Nor do we merge them into indistinction – a bland, fuzzy or murky ambivalence. Yet it is depressive ambivalence or multivalence that is the potential soil of such thinking, allowing distinctions to emerge and take shape in our awareness as wordless feelings and impressions before casting them into words. Schizoid thinking on the other hand achieves disambiguation by challenging the psyche to yield itself in terms of pre-conceived dichotomies, and thus also to yield to and 'prove' these dichotomies. As Melanie Klein argued, the 'depressive position' marks the collapse of this schizoid thinking.

19. The Total Devaluation of Being
— "only a god can save us"

Today, Freudian psychoanalysis, like Marxist socialism before it, is on the road to disintegration. That does not mean that it is dead – though Freud, its god, is long dead. It means that it is no longer an integrated body of thought or a unified practice. This is not just a question of it having developed and in this development split into various schools – Freudian, Kleinian, Lacanian, Jungian, 'independent' etc. It is that the world has changed. The universal domination of a culture of technology – anticipated by Heidegger – is only now reaching its apogee. This is a culture that is hostile to any sense of mystery, anything beyond the control and manipulation of the ego, any understanding of human being that cannot be reduced to formula or panacea, any type of wisdom that cannot be reduced to a set of programmable skills and learnt through a linear step by step training.

The way of thinking that characterises it is *reductive translation*. Economics is reduced to competition, education to training and ethics to moral or religious principles – to laws, rights and duties. Knowledge is reduced to information and trainable skills. Human beings are reduced to a stock of individual 'human resources' whose value is their usefulness in commercial competition. Today's 'technological era' is the era of the *total devaluation of being*.

Technology and commerce are not evils in themselves. What is wrong is the treatment of human beings themselves as managed resources and programmable instruments of commercial growth. For the individual too, is expected to treat their own being as an object of planned self-manipulation for 'personal growth' and 'development'- in the service of increased productive performance. The tool here is 'psycho-technology'. This takes the form of countless self-help formulae and techniques, elating the ego with the prospect of total manipulative control over itself and others through the programming or reprogramming of mind and body. And yet 'positive mental attitude' or 'neuro-linguistic programming' (NLP) cannot fulfil the human will to meaning and the search for individual value fulfilment. The will to meaning is not the will to personal or corporate success and competitiveness. It is rooted in a fundamental openness to the mystery of being. This mystery is anathema to today's 'knowledge capitalists' and 'information technologists'. The search for value fulfilment is not the search for 'value-adding' services and skills. It is rooted in a fundamental awareness of one's own intrinsic values and the intrinsic values embodied by others. This is a awareness foreign to most commercial training consultants and management gurus.

Values are not trainable or tradable. They cannot be added or subtracted. They belong to our essential being. They can be fulfilled and materialised only by first being embodied. Attending a talk or training course on business ethics or integrity, in which values are discussed and their importance explained, does not mean that these values are embodied. To embody a value is not the same thing as to verbally define or promote it. Values cannot be 'instilled' by 'value statements' nor can we learn to embody them through linear, step by step training procedures. All such training achieves is to split mind and body – programming people mentally to act as if they embodied particular values – 'perform' them and thus to appear to enhance their 'performance'.

Authentic integrity, confidence and teamwork, the capacity to *be* and be *with* others – to appreciate and learn to embody oneself the values that another individual *intrinsically* bears within them. NLP was created by abstracting and objectifying the *intrinsic values* embodied by a number of individual therapists – people with embodied presence and a deeply-rooted capacity to be and be with others. Their way of relating to others was then reduced to a toolkit of lifeless and impersonal techniques, justified by a 'scientific' language which reduces human beings to a manipulable set of clearly defined linguistic and perceptual modalities. Such comprehensive and illuminating clarity on how people 'work' and how to control one's personal and social destiny, constitutes a total blindness to the meaning of life and its challenges. It may boost ego confidence but it reveals no understanding of what it means to 'con-fide' in oneself – to have faith in one's own value and values as a human being. This is a faith in something essentially nameless and beyond the ego's control.

Like other philosophies of positive thinking, NLP offers well-being and worldly gain with the minimum of pain. Psychoanalysis on the other hand, partly due to its own philosophical weaknesses, seems to an increasing number of people to offer pain but no gain. The variety of competing approaches to self-understanding and self-improvement, personal health, growth and therapy today are essentially distinguished only by their relation to two major questions. One is the issue of 'pain' and 'gain'. The other issue is whether man can or should make himself into the *object* of his own linear and reductive technological framework of thinking. Doing so would finally elevate the *subject* that controls this object – the ego – to a godlike status. The desire to do so is impelled by fear – for whilst successfully accomplishing its technological domination of the earth by reducing it to a stock of resources for control and exploitation, and whilst successfully reducing knowledge and thinking to the disposal of ready-to-hand 'information', the ego still feels threatened by an inner awareness of the essentially *illusory* nature of this control – and of the unpaid debt it accumulates in exerting it.

This debt is not only an environmental or social debt. Nor is it even an 'existential debt' – the loss of meaning which Viktor Frankl described as 'existential vacuum.' It is an ontological debt or guilt (*Schuld*) – a debt to one's own being. For Heidegger, guilt and its counterpart – the call of conscience – are the natural response of our own self-being to the way we sacrifice our capacity to be ourselves to the unchallenged idols of technology – to self-control, self-management and self-marketing. Time itself ceases to be a space in which to be and find meaning and richness in being, but a resource to be 'used' productively. But if we no longer know how to grant ourselves time to be, we are no longer capable of granting time to be with another human being or to be there for them – to *listen*. We lose the capacity for what Martin Buber called essential relating.

"In an essential relation,...the barriers of individual being are breached and a new phenomenon appears which can appear only in this way: one life open to another – not steadily, but so to speak attaining its extreme reality from point to point, yet also able to acquire form in the continuity of life; the other becomes present not merely in the imagination or feeling, but in the depths of one's substance, so that one experiences the mystery of the other being in the mystery of one's own."

Buber was fiercely critical of Heideggerian ontology, seeing it as a philosophy which sought salvation from ontological guilt in 'self-being' rather than being with others. Yet Buber, like Heidegger spoke an 'ontological' language – a language (*logos*) of being (*ontos*). He rejected all reductionism and reductive translation, holding instead to what is fundamental and essential to human being and relating. Like Heidegger he presented an *essential translation* of terms such as 'guilt' and 'conscience' in terms of human *Dasein* – what it means to 'be there':

"When I answer the call of present being – 'Where art thou?' – with 'Here am I', but am not really there, that is, not with the truth of my whole life, then I am guilty. Original guilt consists of remaining with oneself. If a form and appearance of present being moves past me, and I was not really there, then out of the distance, out of its disappearance, comes a second cry, as soft and secret as though it came from myself: 'Where were you?' That is the cry of conscience."

Buber's is an ontology of the essential 'I-Thou' relation, understood as a dialogue of being. He saw Heidegger's ontology as 'monological' – to do simply with a solitary being one-self. Medard Boss, on the other hand, saw in Heidegger's thinking the basis for an *ontological refoundation* of medicine, psychiatry, and psychoanalysis – an essential translation of human being that explores not only what it means to 'be oneself', but also to 'be with others' (Mitsein), to 'be a body' or 'body oneself' (*leiben*) and to 'go on being' in Beckett's and Winnicott's sense.

Buber's 'ethical' or 'relational' ontology, I believe, is essential to this ontological refoundation, contributing to an essential refoundation of Heideggerian ontology itself. In his account of the 'essential relation' Buber does indeed breach Heidegger's own reduction of *being with* to 'concern', 'care' or 'solicitude'. In accord with Heidegger, on the other hand, he acknowledges that 'self-being' is the basis of *being with*.

"One must truly be able to say 'I' in order to know
the mystery of the Thou in its whole truth."

Today, this 'I' is a psychotic inflation of the ego and its techno-power – an ego, which, at the mere press of a button, can start a computer game or release computer-guided missiles. At the same time psychosis is externalised in the form of 'evil' foreign powers and terrorists. Whilst the West passes judgement on these powers it supplies them with arms and develops the technology of wars. It's solution to actual violence is 'virtual' violence – acted out in films and computer games or through missile technologies which makes real war seem like a mere game, which distance the killer from the killed.

'Mental' psychosis, psychosis experienced internally rather than acted out by terrorists or military technologists, is shunned or shunted about in the 'community' – or else treated only as a potential source of violence (the astonishingly rare violence of the mentally ill). No-one really knows what to 'do' with the mentally ill, because so few know how to *be* with someone who suffers 'mentally'. Above all, no-one wishes to see this suffering as more than just 'mental' or 'emotional' – to see it as the symptom of an *ontologically* sick, neurotic and psychotic world. The reduction of social ontology to individual psychology or biology – to genetics – can in no way bring us to an understanding of their essential dynamics. Gene technology is no substitute for an ontology of values and human relating.

Heidegger's words 'only a god can save us now' can be reformulated to address the current situation of those movements such as psychoanalysis and socialism, which see truth as a dialogue rather than as process or product, the individual as a social being and not an economic atom – 'only ontology can save them now'. In contrast to technological thinking – reducing all relationality to an 'I-It' relation – Buber and Heidegger practiced and demonstrated an ontological way of thinking, characterised not by 'reductive translation' but by 'essential translation'.

An *ontological refoundation* of psychoanalysis cannot but take as its starting point Heidegger's ontology of 'language and being'. This must be extended to embrace and develop Buber's *relational ontology* and its dialogical ethics – the ethics of the 'essential relation'. But the essential relation is also a relation of essences – of each individual's essential 'language of being' – what Bollas calls their 'idiom' or 'aesthetic'. Dialogue is also a dialectical interplay of these idioms, not as cultural or linguistic idioms, but as individual languages of being.

The practice of 'essential translation' and of 'essential relation' both involve a recognition of these languages of being, and an understanding of their relation to the mother tongue and mother culture. For today, the nation state and national languages and cultures are also under threat. To the individual, this can feel like a further devaluation of being, for it is a loss of those symbols of selfhood which the ego requires in order to feel some sense of identity transcending itself. The danger is not that a particular language such as English or Chinese, replaces other languages, but that all languages are sacrificed to the reductive language of technology and commerce, one which has no need for an 'essential translation'. Nations and cultures, like individuals, need neither protect their separate languages and identities nor sacrifice them to a grand merger. They need to translate the essential truth and value of what is 'idiomatic' in other cultures – and learn how to absorb and embody these truths and values in their own idiom.

20. Beyond Interpretation
—the process of 'essential translation'

In translating a word or phrase from one language to another, we ordinarily assume that the meaning of the word in the original language is clear and well-definable. The question is only how it can be translated. The translator's task, then, is to find a word or phrase of equivalent meaning in the second language. This assumption was questioned by Heidegger. He saw thinking itself as a process of translation – of translating a given language into its own words. This is a process familiar in counselling – a client may be asked what they mean by certain words or what certain words mean to them. They are asked to translate their own words using words of their own language. Put differently, they are asked to translate their own customary 'language' – their way of speaking- into different words, but words which also belong to their language.

Philosophy too, involves asking what particular words mean. An example is Heidegger and Buber's discussion of the meaning of 'guilt'. Philosophy questions the automatic assumption that we know what the words of our own language mean, and probes the meaning of a whole variety of words including the word 'meaning' itself. And yet there is an essential difference between this philosophical questioning and simply asking what words mean. Heidegger and Buber did not simply ask what the word 'guilt' means. They asked the question 'What *is* guilt?' To say what a word means, either a foreign word or a word in our own language, is not simply to take recourse to a dictionary or to define it in our own words. It is to ask ourselves what it is that the word essentially names. The question 'what does 'guilt' mean', is translated into a different question: 'What *is* guilt?'. Language and being, meaning and truth are not separated. To question the meaning of language is also to seek the *truth of being*. So also, in listening to a client, the counsellor does not merely seek the meaning of their words but the truth of their being.

In previous chapters the philosophical question was 'What is listening?' That is to say both the meaning and truth of the verb 'to listen' has been sought. Other words such as 'hearkening' and 'heeding' were employed in order to try and say what listening essentially is, what its truth is. This is an example of what it means to seek an *essential translation* of the *word* 'listening'. Essential translation is not just a definition or translation of meaning. It is a process of questioning which seeks to name the truth or essence of something that *is*, in words other than the original.

There are three inseparable but distinct processes involved in essential translation. The first is a process familiar to counsellors – asking what a word means to a person or what they mean with it. In this way the counsellor seeks to elicit not only the personal meaning or definition but the personal truth of a word – the dimension of a person's being that it names. A psychotherapist once described the way she listened and responded to her clients in the following terms. She said that it was as if the client was reading aloud from a text whose language was foreign to the therapist. In doing so the client was translating this text into a language shared with the therapist, but not in words which made complete sense. By questioning what clients meant by certain words or statements, the therapist felt she was encouraging them to dig deeper into the meaning of their text and translate it better – not just for the therapist but for themselves. It is an excellent metaphor of therapy as a *counselling process* – one in which the listener does not seek in any way to 'interpret' a client's meaning of feelings but to help them to 'describe their own experience' and 'get closer to their own feelings'. This does not mean that the counsellor refrains from using their own words to 'reflect' or 'reformulate' what a client is trying to say. Such words are offered in order to help clients in their work of translation, to help them feel understood and supported, and, last but not least, to help the counsellor feel sure that they have properly understood the 'text'.

The second, more philosophical process involved in essential translation quests the trans-personal truth of a word. This is the truth or dimension of being that it essentially names, not just for an individual, but in general – in essence. In this book the words 'hearkening' and 'heeding', 'holding' and 'handling', 'with-holding' etc., were used to translate the essence of what it means 'to listen'. These are not different words for four separate things. Nor are they different words for one 'thing' we call 'listening'. They name four distinct but inseparable aspects of what it is that we call 'listening'. This is not a 'thing' so much as an activity, a process and a practice. Each of these words helped to understand the essence of what listening is. But to understand what anything is in its essential being, means understanding it in relation to being. The four words helped to understand listening as a communication of being. To do so the very word 'being' was used quite a lot. As a philosophical process, essential translation calls upon a language of 'being'. Thus the essence of 'pain' is understood as an apartness from, or separation within, our own being. The essence of 'relating' is understood as 'being with'. The essence of 'conscience' as the 'call of being'. 'Questioning' as a 'questing' of our being, etc. Using the language of 'being' in this way helps us to understand both the 'truth' of being and what it 'means' to be. It is philosophy as 'ontology' – the *logos* of *ontos* or the 'language' of 'being'.

The third dimension of essential translation seeks the *inter-personal* meaning and truth of words. This aspect of meaning and truth is addressed in the psychoanalytic interpretation of 'transference' and 'counter-transference'. The essence of Philosophical Counselling is essential translation, not just as a philosophical process but as a counselling process *and* as a 'psychoanalytic' process. The phrase 'essential translation' is itself an essential translation – an ontological translation of the truth and meaning of what is called the 'analytic' and 'interpretative' process. The practice and process of Philosophical Counselling combines the practices and processes of counselling, philosophy and psychoanalysis – not eclectically but in their *essence*.

To understand the inter-personal dimension of meaning that psychoanalytic theory and practice address, we need to transcend the ontology of 'language and being' and recognise that truth of being lies in what Buber called the 'essential relation' – a relation *between* beings. This intrinsic relationality of being, I believe, can only be fully understood as the interplay and *mutual translation* of what I have called the individual 'languages of being'.

The recognition that each of us not only 'has' or 'speaks' a language but *is* a language is central to this dimension or level of essential translation. Languages are *ways of speaking*. Ways of speaking, however, are ways of making way for meaning. Ontologically, beings are *ways of being*. Ways of being are ways for beings to be – their link with Being. Ways of beings are the ways and 'waying' of Being. In letting themselves and each other be in their own way, they make a way for Being. An individual's 'language of being' is the way in which, in making way for meaning in language, we make way for ourselves to be. It is not the 'text' that the counsellor helps the client to translate. It is the way in which each of us as individuals *translates* our own emotional, experiential and existential 'text' – not only into ways of speaking but into a *way of meaning* and a *way of being*. The translation of a language text can be more or less true to the 'meanings' that the original expresses. The original is itself a translation – the author's way of translating themselves into language, their way of speaking and the idiomatic meanings this makes way for.

Analytic interpretation is a translation of someone's emotional, existential or experiential life text. This can also be more or less true to the original. For the original is itself a translation – not only of the individual's way of speaking and the meanings it expresses, but the individual's way of being and the values this *embodies*. To listen only for a client's conscious or unconscious 'meanings' misses the point. For in quite general terms to genuinely **heed** another person is not only to listen for, understand, interpret or help to translate the meanings ('conscious' or 'unconscious') that a client seeks to express in words but to hear the *value* that this person seeks to embody – the way of being they seek. We cannot hear through to a person's values without respecting and valuing them. And yet just 'respecting' is not enough. For to respect or value someone means to hear through to the value which they seek to embody and fulfil through their way of being. To find value in what someone embodies, their way of being, is not the same as liking or disliking them. An individual's way of being – their 'language of being' – is more than just their way of speaking, their way of translating themselves into language. And yet it includes their way of speaking and meaning.

To find meaning in what somebody says is not just to hear their meaning but to let ourselves be the one who is 'unconsciously' meant. By allowing ourselves to be meant, we acknowledge that 'meaning' is more than the representation of an objective content, but that to mean *something* is also to intend *someone*. Langs regarded awareness of the unconscious communication of the client as central to the listening process of the analysis. We can then hear in the client's words a metaphorical answer to our own unspoken questions. But the 'silent questions' that Langs refers to are not just verbal questions that we refrain from voicing. They are also the essential *questing* of our own being for value fulfilment. To heed someone's 'unconscious communication' is not only to hear a deeper level of meaning in their words. It also means to value the qualities of being that they embody – to find value for oneself in their 'language of being'.

Meanings are expressive potentials of language. Values are embodied potentials of being. The essence of a value is not a verbally prescribed 'moral value' but an emotional quality of being. In speech we identify with the *verbal symbols* of these emotional qualities – thus imbuing words with subjective meaning. In 'projective identification' (Klein) we identify with the *material symbols* of values – thus imbuing things with subjective meaning.

The effort of translating a text from one language into another brings out hidden potentials in our own language – but only if we open ourselves to the foreign language as a distinct and idiomatic *way of meaning*. Similarly, the effort and challenge of translating the essence of another person's 'text' helps us to fulfil the hidden potentials of our own being – but only if we appreciate the distinctness and value of their idiom, the values or qualities of being that they embody in their way of being. To ask a 'silent question' is also to be the question – to be open in our being to the values embodied by another individual. It means being prepared to acknowledge these values also as 'answers' – as a response to the questing of our own being. Conversely, it is through the client's openness to the values embodied by the counsellor, analyst or therapist that he or she is healed or wholed. For these embodied values underly all intellectual, emotional or intuitive capacities or skills.

Langs' understanding of the listening process is a true one: ask a silent question and hear a silent answer. Through **with-holding** verbalisation of the question you will find that what the client says constitutes a symbolic or 'unconscious' answer. But a listening agenda that seeks to analyse and interpret 'meanings', even one that seeks only to help the other to translate their own meanings, can be *devaluing* to a client if it is not complemented by a receptivity to embodied values. 'I respect your being' and 'I hear your meaning' does not mean 'I hear, receive, and thank you for the qualities I perceive in your way of being'. Helping someone to acknowledge and express their true meaning is not the same as helping someone to acknowledge and embody their true values – to find a way of speaking and a way of being that is true to these values. To do so means *valuing* these values.

'Valuing' is the third dimension of philosophical counselling as 'essential translation', its *ethical* rather than purely philosophical or counselling dimension. As such it has to do with the very essence of professional ethics. For a therapist, counsellor or analyst to value a client does not just mean acknowledging the 'exchange value' of the client's payments for sessions. Nor is it a matter of the 'use value' of the client – the insights achieved in working with a particular client. Valuing means understanding the learning achieved in working with a client as something which is in part a learning *from* the client.

Values are *essential* qualities and potentials of being which we translate into *existential* realities – embody in our *way* of being, express in our *way* of speaking and materialise in our life-world. Values 'matter' because they are what is essentially materialised and embodied in matter. The value that a work of art materialises cannot be reduced to a message of meaning. It is connected with the *manner* in which it is materialised – this composer's way of composing, that painter's way of painting, an actor's way of acting etc.

Each specific client, like any human being, can not only receive something from us but also tell us something and give us something. Valuing means being open to what a person gives us simply be being the way they are – acknowledging the value we can find in their way of speaking and way of being. In this way we acknowledge the values that they too, may be seeking to more fully acknowledge and live out. Valuing in this sense is the deepest, most essential level of acknowledgement one can give to another human being. It requires that we too 'translate' the essential values we find expressed in another individual's way of being – that we find a way to express, embody or materialise these essential values in our own existence. By existentially translating and living out what another person 'essence' gives us (embodying as well as 'interpreting') we enrich our own 'language of being'.

This 'will to receive' belongs to the essence of listening, as does the will to impart our own values to others. The job of the therapist is not to interpret or expound their own values in words and impose them on a client. But a therapist who does not seek to consciously *embody* these values in their way of being with a client is not listening or communicating with their whole being. Only by consciousness of what we are saying to someone 'between the lines' – of how we intend our words to speak to them and touch them in their being – can we then gauge their own listening receptivity. Their receptivity not just to the message which we communicate from our being but their receptivity to messages of their own being. Similarly, it is only by consciously embodying their own most essential values or qualities of being that a therapist can gauge the client's own capacity for essential translation – for acknowledging and embodying their own essential values. That is why, for the therapist, essential translation must go together with embodied listening – a way of listening in which the therapist embodies and communicates their own being.

The values which the client seeks to fulfil in their lives will invariably be related to those which the therapist embodies and communicates – and vice versa. A relationship only exists when two or more people form a bond through certain shared values, even though they may each express and embody these values in different ways and with different words and behaviours. Values are like the shared electrons that orbit both atoms in a molecular bond, and create a common electro-magnetic field. The values shared in a human bond create a 'bipersonal field' uniting two individuals.

Atoms either receive or donate electrons to the molecular bond. Unlike atoms, however, each partner in a human bond has a 'valency' which allows them both to donate particular values to the shared 'bipersonal field' and receive certain values from it. The chemistry that connects people, therefore, has to do not only with the values they already embody but with those they don't. The latter are like electron 'holes'. They are 'negative' values – unfulfilled values and unrealised potentials for being. 'Valuing' is a receptivity of the therapist to those *positive* and embodied values of the client which 'fill a hole' for the therapist – correspond to the therapist's own negative or un-ful-filled values. 'Embodied listening' is the embodied communication of those specific positive values of the therapist which correspond to – and therefore genuinely *respond* to – a client's negative values and valency. For these positive values of the therapist embody the client's own un-ful-filled qualities and potentials for being.

Valuing and *embodied listening* are both aspects of *essential translation*, for in order to receive values from another we need to translate them into our own language of being and in order to donate or communicate our values to another we need also to 'speak their language' and thus receive its values. For to 'speak someone's language' means not only to appreciate the type of language they understand, and learn to speak this language. It also means valuing another person's 'language of being' and learning to 'speak' in this language, to receive and embody its values. 'Essential translation' is thus the essential *dialectic* of 'essential relating' – of an ethical *dialogue* of being.

Other people *embody* our own 'negative values' as they also *express* our own unspoken thoughts and feelings. To the extent to which we remain unconscious of negative values however, we experience them as *emotions*. These emotions will be negative if we negate the values underlying them – devalue them. Even positive emotions, however can be the result of dis-identification from values. Language is the instrument of both devaluation and dis-identification. One way of dis-identifying with a value is linguistic 'displacement' – identifying it as the private property of another – as 'yours' or 'theirs'. In this way we deny their essence as shared values, shared potentials and qualities of being. Another way of verbally dis-identifying with a value is quite literally to 'give it a bad name', to pejoratively label a particular quality of being. Or to give it a good name – to idealise it and yet externalise it. What is called 'projection' is the *symbolic externalisation of a value*. The combination of displacement and judgement generates the whole spectrum of 'emotions'. Admiration and envy are both forms of displacement. Fear and hatred arise from a combination of displacement and judgement, as do idealisation and love. Grief and mourning both express the loss of a displaced value – one symbolised by someone or something else. This is paradoxical, for it is precisely through separation from, or loss of, *symbolic values* that we come to appreciate and embody the *essential values* underlying those symbols. The loss of a loved one who symbolised a particular quality of being for us often triggers a process by which we come to acknowledge the 'value' of this quality in ourselves – to internalise its essence. This internalisation process should not be confused with 'introjection'. The psyche 'introjects' value symbols – symbolic values. Essential values become part of our *being* — but only when we free them from symbols and instead experience and embody them as nameless qualities of our being. Not as emotions but as *feeling tones*.

The basic stance of psychoanalysis is that each individual confronts a realm of unconscious thoughts, emotions and desires which may reveal themselves through particular neurotic of psychotic patterns. The basic stance of the counsellor or psychotherapist is also that people need help in coming to terms with their emotions and expressing them freely. Philosophical Counselling acknowledges a third and more basic dimension of human being beyond 'thoughts and feelings', 'reason and emotion'. This is the dimension of positive and negative values and of value fulfilment. We may value a person for their sense of humour or compassion, their courage or calm, their loyalty or adventurousness. We do so not because the person in question advocates these qualities but because they embody them in a particular way. It is the irreducible individual quality in a person's sense of humour or compassion that we value. This irreducible individual quality is the essential value they embody. To value a person because they 'have' a sense of humour is one thing. In this case we do not value the person but a generic quality – having a sense of humour. To value the person is to value the unique and essential quality that they embody in their sense of humour – or even in their depression, despair, sickness or neurosis. The generic quality or value – the sense of humour or compassion – is one expression or translation of a more essential value or quality of being. But we can perceive and receive the essential values that an individual embodies only by first embodying our own.

Value fulfilment is related to the 'will'. Not the will to succeed, to have or to do, nor even the 'will to meaning', but the will or desire to be – to embody our potentials for being. We cannot get or do what we want without first being the sort of person we want to be – even if this means being the sort of person who could do or have certain things. The ego reverses this relation, making being who we want dependent on getting or doing. Even philosophies of 'positive mental attitude' support the ego's will to achieve rather than the will to be.

21. Listening, counselling and psychoanalysis — 'being there' and 'being with'

A philosophical understanding of the terms 'counselling', 'therapy' and 'analysis' can neither merge these three terms into a single 'thing' nor see them as naming three entirely separate and independent things. The term 'philosophical counselling' would itself be a misnomer if, by 'counselling', we understood something entirely separate from psychoanalysis and psychotherapy, or something which merely blurs the boundaries between counselling, analysis and therapy. It would also be a misnomer if we understood 'philosophical counselling' merely as a particular type of counselling – on a par with 'psychodynamic' or 'rational emotive' counselling. Philosophical Counselling cannot be reduced to an 'approach' to counselling, analysis or therapy. For the very term 'philosophical' implies a search for the essence of what it means to be a counsellor, analyst or psychotherapist. This in turn is only possible by looking at the specific philosophical assumptions that are already embedded in the different approaches to counselling, therapy and analysis and questioning the various implicit philosophies that distinguish and unite these practices. This is not merely a matter of examining the theoretical models that govern them but of discerning the basic stance of the practitioner and the *model that this presents* to the client, patient or analysand.

The prototypical 'counsellor', for example, presents to the client not only a model of someone empathic, patient, accepting and non-judgemental but also someone who is *always in control of themselves and who smoothly and professionally enacts a specific social role*. The implicit 'philosophy' this conveys to the client is not only that it is OK to acknowledge and express feelings but also that one can *stay in control* whilst doing so. The philosophical model of health conveyed by the counsellor is that of a person who is in touch with their feelings *and* in control – able to maintain their ego-identity and productively relate through a professional role.

Much the same can be said of the prototypical psychoanalyst. Here, however, there are additional philosophical messages to the client. One message is that health demands some capacity to articulate unconscious processes, to represent them symbolically in words and images. The psychoanalyst presents to the client a model of someone capable of representing unconscious processes in words and images or eliciting such representations from others. Here too there is also a message that says 'you can stay in control'. The basic message of Freud – 'where Id was, the Ego shall be' – affirms that the ego can 'work through' unconscious contents and processes *in order to objectify them and free itself from them.*

The theoretical stances that distinguish different types of psychotherapy whether 'psychodynamic', 'body-oriented' or 'humanistic', all share one thing in common with counselling and psychoanalysis. They each present themselves as essentially rational or scientific. This has important implications, for it means that the practitioners, whatever their 'training' or 'approach', ground their practice in *reason or rational science.* But a theory and practice grounded in 'reason' is not the same as a theory and practice grounded in *being.* And a practitioner whose practice is grounded in reason and the rational understanding of psychological processes is not necessarily *grounded in their own being.*

"The *person* becomes conscious of himself as participating in being, as being-with, and thus as a being. The *ego* becomes conscious of himself as being this way and not that. The person says 'I am'; the ego says, 'That is how I am.'" (Buber)

In our commercial and technological culture, people have lost touch with their own being – with what it means to be themselves and to be with others. Groundedness in being is a stance that is normally identified not with counselling, therapy or analysis but with mystical Eastern philosophies and with esoteric practices such as Zen meditation. Heidegger's service to Western thinking was to have rescued 'therapeutic ontology' from its fashionable 'sixties' association with Eastern mysticism, gurus and meditation. Instead he recollected its roots in the Greek language and philosophy – just as Buber recollected its roots in the Hebrew language and Judaic ethics.

Therapeutic ontology explores what it means to 'be oneself', to 'be there' and to 'be with' others in an authentic way. The 'stance' of the philosophical counsellor is quite simply to authentically be there and be with the client – not as a 'trained' or 'qualified' professional, listening and responding in role, not as a god or expert, not as interlocutor, but as an incarnate, embodied and mortal human being – one addressed in his or her being by the same fundamental questions and dilemmas that affect the client. One whose reasoning ego is grounded in their own being and not vice versa.

Learning to listen means learning to be with another person in silence. Not in order to 'make' them feel comfortable, to 'engage' them, or to 'get to know' them. Not in order to play a role, put on a face or an act. Nor to 'just be' – like a group of people who are each engaged in solitary meditation. Many people have never experienced what it means to be with someone – and thus to listen or be truly heard by another. For them the expression 'to be with someone' implies either an indifferent and contactless proximity or a purely sexual contact – with or without intimacy.

'Being with' has two basic intonations – to **be** with and to be **with.**

Being with another person means being fully present to oneself. Then we can fully 'be there' with the other. 'There', not just as a mind but also as a body and with our whole being. Not as a colleague or acquaintance, helper or counsellor, friend or partner, husband or wife – but as who we are in our essence and in our totality. Not as a separate being, an illusorily detached observer, however 'spiritual', 'caring', 'helpful' or well-meaning. Nor in order to merge our being with the being of another – dissolving our self-being into an anonymous and equally illusory unity. 'Being there' with the other is to truly 'list-en' with our whole being and relate from it.

This 'there' is not a place in me or in the other. Being there does not mean wandering in my own thoughts or feelings in reaction to the thoughts and feelings of another. Nor does it mean leaving myself and my body behind to 'identify' with another. We need to stay with ourselves in order to **be** with another. Yet for many professional counsellors, therapists or analysts being with a client means maintaining professional ego-identity and staying with their own thoughts and feelings only in a detached way. They become someone else than who they are to themselves in their personal life and relationships – with all their ups and downs, moods and crises. 'Being there' is reduced to being present to the client in a 'here and now' which excludes what *has been* and *is to come* in their own lives – the mood they woke up in, the dream they had last night, the unresolved conflict with a colleague or partner that continues to hang over them, the conference they need to attend on the weekend. They assume that to admit the *concrete totality* of their being into the therapeutic relationship would be to let their personal problems and fallibilities intrude into this relationship – preventing them from being there *for* the client. Therefore they dis-identify with the concrete totality of their being and identify instead with their professional persona. This stance reflects a fundamental misconception. For to admit the concrete totality of our being – to be there as a real person – does not mean to be mentally or emotionally preoccupied with one's own existential problems and challenges and therefore incapable of being there *for* and *with* the other. It means allowing our existential and emotional situation – where we are in our life – to *suffuse and colour* our bodily self-experience and feeling tone, our state and tone of being. In this way we do not preoccupy ourself with our own existential and emotional problems, we do not identify with them or dis-identify from them, but remain in touch with them in an embodied way. We ground our 'here and now' in an embodied state of being in which we are in touch with the fundamental questions and dilemmas that underlie our own emotional and existential issues – questions and dilemmas which are shared with all human beings, including our clients. We allow ourselves to *be human*, not by dwelling on our personal problems but by *letting be* our own fallibility, failures and 'fallen' state.

'Fallenness' is allowing ourselves to fall from our godlike status as detached egos or professionals. To 'fall' is to respond to the pull of the ground – the pull of our own being – in a bodily way. In other words, to be who we are – not as a detached ego or psyche but as a mortal human being and as a body. To be a body is to be in touch in a bodily way with the totality of one's being. To 'be' is also 'to dwell' in this body – to take time to linger and sojourn. This is not the same thing as dwelling on our own existence of emotions. To be with others we need to be in touch with ourselves in a bodily way. Being some-body does not mean being a rational ego, or a person with 'professional' role and status. It means being a body and embodying who we are. This involves allowing ourselves to 'fall'. We cease to anchor our being in role, ego-identity or reason, and instead 'drop anchor' within ourselves. We adopt a stance in which we take our stand, not on fluctuating rational or emotional 'grounds', but on the firm ground of our *embodied state and tone of being*. The *gravitas* of the counsellor, analyst or therapist, their capacity to ground themselves in their own bodyhood, is essentially a capacity to bear the weight of their own mortality and that of the client. This means approaching the encounter with another human as if it were our last or their last mortal encounter. The acknowledgement of mortality is thus nothing merely intellectual, and nor does it imply a tragic or pessimistic view of life. It ensures that the therapeutic listener is open to, and capable of containing, the underlying life-and-death issues that a client may be confronting or avoiding. Such issues are related to the meaning and value fulfilment that individuals obtain, or fail to obtain, from life. And to the loss of a dimension of value fulfilment already obtained – whether through relationships or work.

Heidegger described authenticity as 'being towards death' – an 'anticipatory resoluteness' that allows us to be, not only in the immediate present, but in a way that allows our own future to beckon us from the ultimate horizon of our mortality. This confrontation with our mortality through being a body is therefore also an opening to our own infinite and awesome potential for being – an encounter with the richness of our own being and the being of the other. Being a body does not mean being 'only' a mortal body, therefore. For just as the essence of language is nothing linguistic but has to do with what is said rather than what is spoken, with meanings rather than words, so too is the essence of our bodyhood nothing merely physical or biological. We do not have bodies, we body. Being a body means bodying who we are. Through our bodies we embody and body forth our own values, our qualities of being. Grounding ourselves in our bodyhood and facing our bodily mortality put us in contact with that which we embody and body forth. This is our own being with its intrinsic values, qualities and potentials.

Being a body is intimately connected with *being in silence* and *being in touch*. To be able to 'relate' to someone means finding our own way of relating to them – of talking with them, doing things with them and 'getting on' with them. But we cannot relate to someone in this way unless we are capable of being with them in silence. Being in silence is a patient granting of time in which to let things be and in this way come to light in their being. Being silent means allowing ourselves to be more than just a face and a social person. To be silent is to fully be a body. Only in this way can we be more than just a simple body but be some-body – be ourselves. This is not the same as needing to do something with our bodies – to talk, gesture and express ourselves physically.

Many people find it unbearable to **be** in silence, because they have not found a way to bear themselves in silence – to be a body rather than a talking head. To be in silence is to *bear* our whole bodily self-awareness in silence rather than bearing it forth in speech or bearing it down by ego-detachment. It is this that allows us to be in intimate touch with ourselves and others. Many fear intimate contact with themselves or others and therefore avoid being in silence. If faced with silence they fidget or adopt awkward physical postures in an attempt to flee their own bodies. They are still present physically in the 'here and now' but only in a dis-embodied way – wandering in their own minds or looking on as detached observers. Although they can still be touched, they are not themselves in touch with their own essential being and cannot reach out to touch the essential being of another. They are not incarnate as beings but only as egos, and fear falling into embodiment.

To be with another is to be-in-touch with the other – to make contact with their essential being. This does not mean touching them physically or with one's words, but touching them with one's essential being. Being 'there' means being at this place of contact between ourselves and another human being. The 'there' is the space that opens up from this contact, the space of the Between. The Between is not the physical space between us. Nor is just a mind-space 'in you' or 'in me', a space in which we project our own fantasies thoughts, and feelings. It is the space of our essential relation – the relation of two human beings who are in contact with each other's essential being. The Between is not an empty space of silence filled only with our own thoughts and feelings – it is the fullness that is still unheard and unspoken, unthought and unfelt – the as yet unknown reality of one's own being and that of the other.

To **be** in silence with another is to communicate silently with your whole being. It does not mean being mute – not talking, not expressing, not relating, not doing- but staying with the underlying silence that lingers beneath all talk and all expressing and doing. The silence of the Between. A lot goes on in this Between, yet many fear that it is empty. They don't give themselves a chance to experience its fullness – to participate in what goes on within it. They need constantly to distract themselves from the silence of the Between or bury this silence in conversation. That is because silence always holds or poses questions. Being in silence means staying with our unstated or unspoken questions, and staying also with the fundamental *questing* of our being for contact with other beings and wholeness of being. Being in silence is connected with the questing of our being and thus with being the question. To be the question is to be open to become the answer – to let it come to us and become part of our being. This answer comes from the Between – if we are there.

This brief elucidation of 'therapeutic ontology' has explored the nature of being there and being with. Being a body and being in silence, being in touch and being the question are some of the essential dimensions of being with. But being there and being with are also the essence of listening. We should therefore expect that the various dimensions of being there and being with are also dimensions of listening. In earlier chapters of this book, the overall theme of Being and Listening was looked at through the 'language of listening' – of **hearkening** and **heeding, holding** and **handling, with-holding** and **hinting.** These keywords echo the same dimensions of *being there* and *being with* which are elucidated here through the 'language of being' – of *being a body, being in silence* and *being in touch.*

The word 'symbol' derives from the Greek *sumballein* – to hold together. Being a body means holding together who we are in a bodily way – free of *mental* symbols. Being in touch means **holding** who we are together with who the other is – neither merging or separating our being from the being of the other but acknowledging a sameness-in-difference and difference-in-sameness. The 'there' is the site of this contact – the Between which both distinguishes and unites two beings in their being. **Holding** is holding together. It goes together with maintaining a particular physical stance and posture, one in which we are simultaneously in touch with ourselves and with the other. Holding is related to **with-holding** speech – with being in silence rather than making 'encouraging noises'. For in speech we do not bear our bodily being in silence so much as body ourselves forth in movement and expression. In so far as the body moves, it speaks. Where there is true listening, the listener is not only silent but still and motionless. Being in silence is also a **hearkening** to that silence – the silence of the Between. Being in touch means that we not only **hold** but **handle** others in this silence. We do so through the unseen movement of our 'listening body' – flexibility of our inner bearing towards them.

Being a body means embodying our whole existential and emotional world in silence – letting it suffuse our bodily self-experience and set the tone of our listening through the tone of our physical presence. The 'mood' or 'tone' of being that we then embody is not something merely 'personal' or 'subjective', an accidental product of our current life-circumstances or of getting out of bed the wrong side. It is also a frequency or wavelength of relationality – one through which we can tune in and disclose synchronous aspects of the other's being. Being allows us to experience our embodied tones of being as antennas – to **hearken** with them.

With-holding immediate response to someone's words allows us to **hearken** to others, to take in or **heed** the meaning of their words in silence, and to heed the values or qualities of being that they embody in silence. These values are only **hinted** at by words, just as our own words are a translation of the values or qualities of being that we embody in silence. **With-holding** also goes together with being the question. This lets other human beings be the answer – allows us to **heed** the way in which they embody our own latent values or qualities of being. **With-holding** and **heeding** prevent us from reacting emotionally or empathising only with our emotions. We acknowledge the other not just as a person with feelings but as some-body important – someone who embodies values that we too can value and embody. Listening is not only a receptivity to what has been said but an active non-representational anticipation of what is yet to be said. In **with-holding** the listener refrains from representing in advance the words which will be spoken but nevertheless anticipates their message – senses, wills and values what they might disclose. Listening is in this sense akin to prayer, to trust and to hope, for these too, are essentially forms of non-representational anticipation – a questing or 'requesting' in which we open ourselves to receiving something of value without imposing our own terms or demands on another.

22. Authentic Speech
— listening and the jargon of 'body language'

It has become a truism of counselling training that people rely more on 'non-verbal' communication and 'body language' to understand each other than they do on words. That this is so is never questioned. Nor why it is so. The distinction between 'verbal' and 'non-verbal' communication ignores the fact that speech is itself a bodily activity, and in this sense a form of 'body language'. Conversely, the gestural codes that distinguish different cultures and sub-cultures, are themselves a form of indirect 'verbal' communication with its own 'words' – a symbolic vocabulary of gestures which may 'mean' different things in different cultural contexts. When a dancer performs a stylised set of symbolic movements, these are based on a particular kinetic vocabulary. Such a dancer is kinetically 'literate' – able to call upon a certain finite vocabulary. That does not mean that they are articulate – able to creatively embody their own being in the language of movement. Articulacy is not a matter of vocabulary alone but of authenticity. An intellectual may be verbally literate to a high degree. That does not mean that they are self-articulate – able to authentically disclose their own being in speech. Someone less verbally literate may be more physically or emotionally self-articulate. The distinction between literacy and articulacy is a crucial one, for if we identify articulacy (verbal, emotional, or physical) with literacy (having a specific vocabulary) authenticity is seen as a monopoly or privilege of the highly-educated. Someone can be emotionally articulate in an embodied way that does not require a great deal of use of emotion words – the conventional vocabulary of 'emotional literacy'. Great composers and musicians seek to forge their own authentic languages of emotional self-articulation which then disclose new dimensions of feeling in their listeners.

'Authenticity' is not a word often used in a counselling context. Instead there is the concept of 'congruence'. Someone's words are regarded as congruent if they accord with their 'body language'. If they say 'I'm fine' whilst trembling with anxiety, sadness or rage this is a sign of incongruence. Congruence, or the lack of it, is seen purely in terms of the relation between someone's words and their body language. This viewpoint has a profound impact on the way we listen. For it implies that there is no sense in which someone's words can, in themselves, be either authentic or inauthentic. It prevents us from listening to people's language as language. The person who says 'I'm fine' whilst trembling with emotion is in essence not saying anything with their words. The words are not, in this sense, 'incongruent' but rather empty. What communicates is not their words but their 'body language'. This does not exclude but includes all the physical features of verbal utterance such as voice and intonation.

What does it mean to listen to someone's words as words, rather than as (bodily) speech. We listen to language as language whenever we read. Superficial, inauthentic writing is empty writing – it does not say anything to us or touch us. The same is true of superficial, inauthentic speech. The words may or may not be incongruent with a person's body language. The fact that they are congruent, however, does not guarantee that they say anything to us or touch us. Words that say something and touch us do so because they do not merely represent something or someone. They are not merely about something or someone, nor do they merely represent something for someone. Words that touch us do so because they are not two-dimensional representations that signify or point to something but more like three-dimensional containers. They say more than they signify. They house more meaning or meaning space within them than appears on the surface. The speaker dwells within them. They are not signifiers. For the speaker they are a *second body*.

Words that merely signal are like items of clothing paraded on a washing line or waved about in one's hand. The speaker does not dwell within them but only flags information with them using a conventional linguistic code. Words that merely signify are like clothes worn because of their designer labels. All fashions are uniforms. Words too, can function as ideological uniforms or straightjackets.

The authenticity of a speaker's words is measured in the same way as the authenticity of a writer's words. The author who flags us with their language is not themselves there within this language, but instead hiding behind it. Authors who squeeze themselves into a prefabricated language constrict themselves with their verbal uniforms. Such authors may be verbose and literate but they are not authentic. To be authentic is to be articulate, to wear words which, like well-fitting clothes do not restrict our articulation and movement but facilitate it. Well-chosen or well-crafted clothes are like a second body. Well-chosen or well-crafted words even more so. Not only because they are our words rather than consciously or unconsciously borrowed phrases. But because in the same way that clothes disclose as well as clothe our bodies, these words disclose as well as clothe our being. The weight attached in our culture to 'non-verbal communication' is a symptom of how few people are able to shape their language in such a way as to experience words as a second body and touch others with their words. The less able people are to find themselves in language the more they rely on body language to communicate. In this they are like actors who compensate for the poverty of a text with dramatic voicing.

Speech can be totally congruent with body language and yet disembodied – lacking substance and fullness. This is because the speaker is no more present in his or her own words than in his or her own body. Children who have difficulty in physical articulation – in finding themselves within their bodies – also have difficulty in verbal articulation – in finding themselves within language. For words to become a second body we need to find ourselves in language, but we can only do this by hearing it speak in a new way – with our bodies and not just our minds. To learn to experience the word as a second body means learning to listen to language with our bodies. Listening to language with our bodies does not mean attending to someone else's voice tone and body language – that is something counsellors are taught to attend to with their minds. Listening to language with the body means **heeding** their words as words – letting them sink in and speak to us. Letting them touch us. Disembodied words, inauthentic words that do not touch us, may carry a great deal of information about a person that may be of interest and importance or not. They may be congruent or incongruent with a person's body language. But what they essentially tell us is that this person has not found themselves in language and therefore cannot have fully found themselves in their own bodies.

Body language that is incongruent with a person's words does not authentically embody the individual. If a person unknowingly fidgets or clenches a fist while speaking this does not mean that the fidgeting or clenching of the fist represents the 'real' person – concealed 'behind' his or her words. For were that individual to have genuinely found themselves in their bodies they would neither speak in a way that is incongruent with their body language nor need to adopt the body language that they do. Paradoxically, the more theoretical and mental attention is focussed on people's body language the less bodily attention we give to each other's language as language – the less we listen to language with our bodies. The less we hear how disembodied a person's language may be. The more we focus on congruence or words and body language the less we hear how disembodied a person may be in both dimensions, even if totally 'congruent'.

Psychology identifies emotional literacy with the capacity to represent our feelings in words or body language – to talk about them or express them physically. Such literacy is far removed from authentic self-articulation, for it involves labelling bodily feeling tones in pre-fabricated or fashionable emotional language. Authentic self-articulation requires that we seek and find our own language in bodily feelings that are our own, seek and find our own bodily feelings in a language that is our own. That we find ourselves in our bodies through language – and vice versa. Technical-commercial culture, education and training, on the other hand, encourage a disembodied use of language as a tool or instrument for communicating and manipulating information.

"Maybe history and tradition will fit smoothly into the information retrieval systems that will serve as resource for the inevitable planning needs of a cybernetically organised mankind. The question is whether thinking, too, will end in the business of information processing." (Heidegger)

The worker in the information age no longer crafts raw materials directly with his tools but merely manipulates these tools themselves – handling and programming the computers, robots and instruments which work the materials. The twentieth century is the century in which language too, has become not only a tool of production but an object and product of manipulation. The ego in the information age does not use language as a tool to handle the raw material of meaning, but instead manipulates the tool itself – language. Words are not a second body but part of the 'language machine'.

"The language machine regulates and adjusts in advance the mode of our possible usage of language through mechanical energies and functions. The language machine is – and above all, is still becoming – one way in which modern technology controls the mode and the world of language as such. Meanwhile, the impression is still maintained that man is the master of the language machine. But the truth of the matter might well be that the language machine takes language into its management and thus masters the essence of the human being." (Heidegger)

The language machine is not a physical machine – a word processor or computer – but a network of social institutions which shape and regulate technological and cultural languages. Education and training institutions of all sorts, whether technical, academic or managerial – and including those which provide training in counselling, analysis and psychotherapy "regulate the mode of our possible usage of language". They do so through the specialist terminologies and phraseologies which they recognise as 'scientific' or 'orthodox'. A trainee psychoanalyst is expected to master the use of a particular Freudian or Kleinian variety of psychoanalytic terminology – and keep to it – just as much as a trainee programmer is expected to respect the proper use of computer jargon.

Any type of knowing that cannot be reduced or fitted into a cultural or technical jargon can find no place in this pluralistic but nevertheless totalitarian network of social institutions. Those who are not psychologically or technically literate – who have not mastered the right 'lingo' are excluded. Not only the uneducated or illiterate, the physically handicapped or clumsy, but also those whose verbal or physical self-articulacy defies institutional convention. Young people are a special problem for social institutions. Their education is increasingly geared to training them in skills and technical jargons – even without their having found themselves in language or in their own bodies. But if the inherent desire of young people for creative self-articulation – physical and verbal – is denied, it is no surprise that one result is illiteracy. Verbal literacy is no longer identified with the power of creative self-articulation but – and with some truth – with conformity to the institutional training machine – the Language Machine. Technical literacy will for some young people provide a substitute for verbal literacy and articulacy. Physical articulacy – sport or physical arts – will do the same for others. Literacy in the traditional sense – the acquisition of a broad vocabulary and its mobilisation in the service of creative self-articulation, will become a preserve of the few. Literacy in the modern sense – the domination of the language machine in all its forms – the media, technology, political, business and institutional languages – will fight a battle with verbal illiteracy and its physical equivalent – inarticulate violence supported by verbal hooliganism. The essence of the language machine is the *language mind* – the experience of language as something purely mental. Without the experience of the word as a second body the physical body and its 'language' becomes an icon and fetish.

23. The 'God project'
— counselling, teaching and counselling training

To nurture authentic listening it is especially important that training in listening and counselling, psychoanalysis and psychotherapy, do not take the prevalent form of indoctrination in theory combined with 'practical' training and exercises i.e. the reduction of being and being with to technical skills – and the reduction of authentic speech to the jargon of 'congruence' and 'body language'. In contrast to the traditional concept of congruence (between mind and body, verbal and non-verbal communication) Charles Curran introduced the notion of *self-congruence*. A Roman Catholic priest as well as a counsellor and language teacher, Curran identified self-congruence with 'incarnation' i.e. embodiment.

"There is.....a kind of continuum going from a non-incarnate state of the 'I' as removed from and unrelated to 'myself', to an incarnate state in which the 'I' embraces and accepts the 'myself'....The first 'I' remains discarnate with the 'myself'. [It] judges and communicates in abstraction and ideals; it resists the concrete and limited self and reality in which the myself must live and function."

Curran found parallels between his work as a psychotherapist and counsellor and the work of a foreign language teacher. Foreign language students regard the teacher as a perfect and fluent speaker and as a language expert at the same time – altogether 'a kind of god figure'. By virtue of their role and the way they are regarded, both the counsellor and teacher are encouraged to identify with the 'I' rather than the 'myself'. This Curran calls the human 'God project'.

"[The] tendency in man to stay related to himself and others in a universal, intellectual mode of communication might be explained...by saying that man has an initial urge in the direction of being infinite rather than finite. It is almost as though, in this God-project, if one cannot be totally God, at least he can be somewhere between man and God. Man takes a risk and chances failure and self-defeat if he lets himself experience his finite condition. The contradiction in this, however, is that he has no sense of personal value and achievement unless he does so. Personal redemption – in the meaning of having acquired a sense of one's personal value and worth – only follows upon personal incarnation."

What Curran writes here about a 'universal, intellectual mode of communication' can be said of representational thinking in general – whether its content is ideational or emotional. 'Incarnation' and the abandonment of the personal God-project allow the language student not only to accept or represent the foreign language in his own familiar and controlled terms – those of the mother tongue – but also to fully receive and embody its 'values' and 'laws', its 'strange' sound-qualities and grammar-rules. Its otherness.

What Curran calls 'redemption' on the other hand is therefore more than just a bland psychological 'acceptance' of self and other in the here and now. Echoing Buber he emphasises that the 'I-myself' congruence allows an 'I-myself-other relationship' and "a very genuine, realistic self-appraisal of what the self is *and can be*." To facilitate the student's or client's personal learning or 'redemption' however, the 'knower' (teacher or counsellor) must take the first step in 'incarnation' – and thus initiate the incarnation-redemption process. This turns the counselling or teaching session into a 'sacrament'. The intent of the knower in this sacrament is to knowingly sacrifice all types of language and behaviour, all communicative safeguards and role supports, which in any way reinforce their apparent omniscience, infallibility and unmarred goodness in the eyes of the client or student. It is this sacrifice which ultimately redeems the student or client, allowing the latter to be who they are and can be rather than clinging to their own ego-identity, ego-omniscience and ego-omnipotence – their God-project.

It is because he brings out the intimate personal learning involved in being a language student Curran speaks not of teachers or counsellors but of 'knowers', not of counselling or learning but of 'counselling-learning'. Counselling-learning is based neither on an impersonal intellectual type of teaching nor on a 'purely' personal type of counselling, but a type of personal learning for both counsellor and client. This concept has implications not only for counselling and teaching but also for counselling training. Here, the central issue is that of authority. For in any system of training the question is – who trains the trainers? From what or who do they derive their authority? On one level the answer to this question is simple – from institutional structures, hierarchies and lineages, which, by their very establishment command a certain respect from trainees and provide a language and logistical framework for the training. Trainers themselves however, are caught between two stools. On the one hand they derive authority and status from the institution and/or its founder and are seen as 'incarnations' of this authority. On the other hand they know intuitively that their real authority as trainers comes from their authenticity – an authenticity that is only achieved by not relying on the god-like status granted them by the discarnate authority of institution, but by being with their trainees in an incarnate and authentic way. This is where the concept of 'training' is misleading, implying the existence of 'expert' trainers whose authority is institutionally pre-established and therefore not dependent on the degree of authenticity they embody in their training. For whilst an institution may admit that the training provided by some of its trainers is 'unsatisfactory', 'mediocre' or even 'bad', the very use of terms such as 'good' and 'bad' misses the point. It misleads the trainers in assessing themselves in terms of their 'performance' and 'results' or through trainee 'feedback' and 'evaluation' – what they do and how well they do it. But this *what* and *how well* are secondary manifestations of something more essential and primary – *who* they are and how they embody themselves.

For the trainee the situation is also dichotomous. As temporary or permanent members of the institution they may accept the authority of their trainer as an 'incarnation' of institutional authority and that of the founder. On the other hand they intuitively evaluate the authority of a trainer in terms of his or her personal authenticity – the trainer's capacity to *be with* them in an embodied and incarnate way rather than hiding behind a jargon, a role and a programme of managed activities. The perceived authenticity of the trainer is above all conditioned by how the trainer *listens* to the trainees – both as individuals and as learners, both pedagogically and personally, both as a trainer and as a counsellor. An authentic teacher of counselling is a counselling-teacher and a counselling-learner – learning about themselves, learning about teaching and learning about counselling.

The false dichotomy of teaching and counselling is at its sharpest in the practice of individual or group 'supervision'. The supervisor must decide at each point whether to listen to the supervisee(s) with their minds or with their whole being, whether to hear the individual supervisee as a student who makes mistakes or as a whole person who needs understanding, whether to respond to them as a teacher or as a personal counsellor or analyst. The paradoxicality of supervision lies in the way these different aspects and dimensions of listening intertwine. This is not merely a particular complication of supervision but the essential and defining paradox of 'counselling-learning' and 'counselling-teaching' in general. Curran's concept of counselling-learning cannot be realised simply by replacing didactic training methods with a 'hands-off' and 'facilitative' training style. In the training of counsellors and psychotherapists we see all too often a separation between authoritative 'input' in the form of reading and lectures, and democratically 'facilitated' group activities in which input is elicited from the trainees. Subjects or topics are 'taught' or 'studied'. Pair and group activities are 'facilitated'. In the first context the focus is on a theoretical rubric and language; in the second on persons. The language by which trainees are taught to frame their understanding of communication is divorced from the language they are expected to use in communicating.

The root assumption in many types of training is that there can be either intellectual discussion or personal encounter, that dialogue must either be topic-centred or person-centred, that statements must either be general statements of opinion about a subject or personal statements addressed to a person, that the group focus must be either 'theoretical' or 'experiential'. This assumption can be challenged both theoretically and experientially. An individual's contribution to a 'theoretical' discussion also carries personal messages from one individual to another. An individual's self-disclosures in an experiential activity also carry theoretical assumptions and pose philosophical questions. If the theoretical language of the training is an adequate one, it can provide an implicit but nevertheless conscious medium of self-disclosure and group interaction. The more profound this theoretical language the more it will provide a linguistic medium that is superior to explicitly 'personal' or 'person-centred' exchanges in cultivating both experiential self-awareness and authentic inter-personal dialogue. The latter both require a conscious awareness of language as a medium of implicit communication between people. Explicit language merely represents people's experience. Implicit language allows them to say something from themselves and say something to one another while talking about themselves or about each other. For it to do so however, they must develop a listening awareness of the richness of implicit communication – the silent messages that are conveyed when people seem on the surface to be only talking about something. They must also develop a listening awareness of language itself – of how the well-chosen and well-crafted word, 'le mot juste' – facilitates and enriches this implicit communication. The purpose of intellectual discussion is to question ordinary language in order to help us find le mot juste. Ordinary personal language, however explicit in its emotionality, can, in contrast, actually diminish the richness and intimacy of implicit communication by imposing stereotyped and unquestioned phraseology. Explicit communication is indirect – we use words to represent our experience rather than speak from it. Implicit communication is direct – we use it to touch others with messages that would be lost or distorted in everyday explicitness.

To facilitate communication is not the same thing as to facilitate dialogue. People can communicate happily without ever questioning what is really going on between them and what is really being said. Dialogue is an attempt to find words which echo and deepen the implicit communication going on between people and thus disclose in an experiential way what the communication is essentially about. To facilitate a dialogue in this sense is not a matter of psychoanalysing or psychologising people's contributions to a discussion in order for them to experience the meaning of a particular psychoanalytic or psychological vocabulary. To do so would be to abandon the search for le mot juste – to assume that one already had it ready to hand and therefore did not need to listen for it. To facilitate a listening dialogue, it is not individuals who need to be explicitly questioned. Language itself needs to be questioned and explored – transformed into the bearer of an inner knowing and into a medium for implicit communication. This is the purpose of the 'listening circle', whose rules involve not addressing questions to other participants directly, and not reacting to another person's words without pausing to first listen inwardly and heed what has been said. The Listening Circle is a structured framework for a non-structured 'counselling-learning', one in which the group can achieve an every closer unity between what is being discussed (the 'It') the words in which it is disclosed, and what is said by one person to another *through* these words (*dia-logos*). The 'We-It' relation becomes a living medium for the 'I-Thou'.

The Christian mythos speaks of the Word become Flesh, the *incarnation* of the Logos in Christ. This can be interpreted in several ways. In the masculine interpretation it is implied that the Flesh, in itself, does not speak – that it has no language, no text, no 'Word' of its own. Thus the Word has first to subordinate the Flesh, to establish the domination of symbolic values – the language mind and the linguistic ego. This is the 'God project' of the ego. It denies that cellular and organic activity, our physical senses and physical movement, are themselves languages – the Word of the Flesh. In the feminine interpretation, the Word becomes Flesh through embodiment or 'incarnation'. Symbolic values and rituals based on the written word are surrendered and sacrificed in order to embody the 'true' or 'divine' Logos – the language of love.

This feminine interpretation sees all holy writ, all sacred texts, as imperfect or distorted translations of a wordless inner knowing that is rooted in our bodyhood. It sees bodyhood as our primary language, language itself as a second body. The Word as such cannot be identified with words and symbols. As the Logos it is the wordless language of faith – of our inner knowing and inner being. This is a language which is embodied or incarnate in the Flesh, one which we can only 'hear' by being a body and attending to our bodily awareness. Understood in this way, the Christian Logos not only echoes the logos of Heraclitus but also values its embodiment and strives to embody it more fully through love. Embodied values are the vocabulary of this logos, not words however moral or religious. The masculine interpretation of the Logos, on the other hand, substitutes words for the Word, verbal language for an embodied Language of Being. It identifies the true Father (Being) with the Son (the linguistic ego or 'I'). The true father is not this glorified 'I'. It is the Pleroma or fullness – the Being of All That Is and All Who Are.

The evaluation of certain ways of being as 'masculine' and others as 'feminine' (masculine aggression vs feminine passivity, masculine intellect vs feminine intuition etc), categorises and displaces qualities which each and every individual can value. It also denies the fundamental distinction between symbolic or named values on the one hand, and essential or embodied qualities of being on the other. There has been, historically, an undeniable tendency for man to identify with symbolic values rather than essential or embodied ones. With the Word as a *textual body of meaning* rather than with the Flesh as the embodiment of the human spirit – its living symbol and text.

When the word ceases to be a second body, its speech is no longer the speech of the breath as psyche and it holds no inner resonance or *logos*. Then we can no longer distinguish its voice and its 'I' – the linguistic ego – from the inner voice of our own being. That is the essential dilemma of all religions of the Word. Their

God speaks and says 'I am', just as mortals do. And yet the little word 'am' speaks of more than just a being. It speaks of Being or 'beingness'. We cannot separate subject and predicate, a divine (or mortal) being that truly 'is' from the very 'beingness' or capacity to be which first allows it (or us) to say 'I **am**'. Religions of the Word are all patriarchal because they are all religions of 'the father'. They each wrestle with an eternal question – the relation between the nameable and the nameless, between the 'I' that is and its source or 'is-ness', between Language and Being. To answer this question they either separate these aspects of divine Being or attempt to merge them. They either name them as separate beings (Son and Father, Logos and Pleroma), or merge them under a single name (Allah or Jahweh).

Speaking and spreading the Word has evolved into vocation of man. But 'woman' means 'one who vibrates' – therefore one who can resonate in attunement with others – who can listen. 'Woman' also means 'the veiled one'. Wo-man relates to language as to a loose but veiling garment – a breathing garment. They can listen beneath it. That is why listening has become the vocation of women and counselling and therapy are seen as 'soft'. Vibrating in harmony and attunement is a property of bodies not of dis-embodied minds. True listening is embodied listening. To be a listener is to be a body. To listen with one's whole being is to listen not just with one's mind but with one's whole body. But there is no concept of the 'listening body' in the religions of the divine Word or divine Father, nor any distinction between essential values and symbolically represented ones. Fatherhood too, is a symbol of divinity.

The Jungian fondness for symbolism notwithstanding, an *essentially feminine* religiosity is free of symbols and symbolic representations. The real mother, embodied in real fleshly women, rules. The Great Mother is 'mother earth' – a living body not a symbol. As soon as there are symbols of femininity – symbolic 'goddesses' – we are no longer dealing with an essentially feminine religiosity but with the symbolic representation of femininity. Identification with symbols is an essential feature of masculine religions. Identification with the body and with bodies is an essential feature of feminine religiosity. Here too, there lies a concealed paradox however. For the essence of the body is itself nothing physical or biological but lies in what it embodies and bodies forth – and that is not a body but a being. Every body is unique because of what it embodies – the values or qualities of being that it translates into flesh and blood. That is why the masculine identification with words and symbolic values is a denial of the body. For it is through the body and that we wordlessly embody our own essential values – our individual qualities of being. And it is through the body that we first are granted the power of the Word – the ability to communicate these values symbolically as 'meanings'. Speech is itself a bodily activity. Listening on the other hand is not mute silence but *virtual speech*. The virtual speech of the listener is not 'inner speech' – a frenetic anticipation and rehearsal of our own words that preoccupies us as we listen. Instead it is we who dwell within the word of the other, as within a second body. We hearken to the silent 'inner word' (*logos endiathetos*) of the other and respond to it from our being.

The virtual speech of the listener does not consist of disembodied mental words we rehearse in our minds. It is a listening awareness of all our potential responses in speech – our potential movements, gestures, utterances and intonations. This potential speech is speech that is not yet fully but still only 'virtually' embodied in physical utterance. And yet it is also speech – it communicates. The mobility, range and depth of our potential responses to one another in speech is the mobility of our listening. This mobility is also the articulacy of our virtual speech, the speech of the listening body. The experience of the word as a second body is the experience of how words, like garments, restrict or free our listening body and its virtual speech – what we feel moved to say. As listeners we 'try on' each other's words as we would each other's clothes. Our listening bodies dwell within the word of the other as within a more or less restrictive, expressive or breathing garment. We sense the 'inside' of each other's verbal clothing, its inner shape and 'feel'. We get a sense both of the sort of person who wears this language and what it does to their inner being.

24. The Knowing Listener
— being and 'bodying'

This book is an attempt to explore the nature of listening in general and of therapeutic listening in particular. To do so, to attempt to think through to the essence of what we call 'listening' is an inherently paradoxical venture. For thinking itself cannot be separated from listening. Thinking is more than just reasoning. It involves what Freud called 'Freier Einfall' – letting things come to one. This implies that we are open to receive what might come to us – that we are listening inwardly. *Freier Einfall* is usually translated as 'free association'. This is not only a mistranslation but a misunderstanding. Mental and verbal associations are not generally free at all but shaped by the language mind and its network of linguistic collocations. To associate 'catch' with 'bus', 'man' with 'woman', 'time' with 'money', 'tomb' with 'womb' is not to freely associate at all. Freier Einfall is an openness to let associations come to us that we would not automatically come to, associations transcend the habitual tracks and junctions of our language mind. The idea of 'free association' begs the question. The question is: how can we to listen inwardly to ourselves in a way that allows us to make genuinely new links and connections, lets genuinely new constellations appear in our mental skies? What sort of listening is it that nurtures thinking? This question closes the circle that links thinking and listening. We want to think the nature of listening and yet to think implies that we already know what listening is for – thinking itself depends on our knowing how to listen and let thoughts come to us which transcend our existing ideas and knowledge.

Put this way the question 'What is listening?' is inseparable from the question 'What is thinking?' and both questions are inseparable from the question 'What is knowing?'. This book has not only attempted to think the essence of listening. It has also claimed knowledge of what listening is and of how to listen. What listening is and how to listen are linked by the notion of authentic listening, for to listen authentically is to listen in a way that is true to the essence of listening. But what is the basis of these or any other claims to know something about listening or to know how to listen 'properly' or 'authentically'? This is not just a philosophical question but one of basic significance in counselling, analysis and psychotherapy. Put in other words it asks 'What sort of 'knowledge' or 'experience' qualify someone to regard their listening as of therapeutic value to others? One common answer is 'self-knowledge'. But one important question that this answer begs is what does it mean to 'Know Thyself'. Psychological or psychoanalytic self-knowledge is knowledge about ourselves. Knowledge about ourselves, including our 'unconscious' feelings, motives and moves, is something that we have or acquire. This is not the same thing as knowing. Knowing is an *activity* not a state.

To want to think about listening conceals the paradox that thinking itself involves listening. Similarly, to speak of 'knowing about listening', or 'knowing how to listen' also conceals an intrinsic paradox. That is because listening itself can be understood as a type of *knowing* and a type of *unknowing*.

Listening is a type of unknowing because it is openness to whatever might 'come to us'. It does not represent, prejudge, or preconceive this in advance, let alone reason it out, calculate or plan it. In this sense it is not a 'mental', 'verbal' or 'rational' activity so much as a wordless and intuitive one. But that is only half the story. Were it the whole story it would be entirely up to our reason or imagination to interpret and make sense of our intuitions – to convert them into representational knowledge. This is the goal of psychoanalysis, which it can be argued, fosters a type of 'knowledge' derived from listening but not intrinsic to it. The basis of this knowledge – the analyst's intellectually and emotionally sharpened observations – is not the analyst's *listening* or *being* as such but the analytic theories which frame and generate these observations as hypothetical interpretations. The analyst 'tests' the hypotheses out with the analysand. The assumed authority of the analyst is the authority of reason and scientific method.

Against this conclusion it can be argued that the authority of the therapeutic listener is grounded in the authority of a different type of knowledge. This type of knowledge is sometimes called 'pragmatic knowledge' or 'tacit' knowledge and expressed in practical activities such as driving a car. This is not a knowledge about but knowing *how*. Pragmatic knowing is a type of knowing that is inseparable from doing. Though people are taught to drive cars, and this teaching includes knowledge about the car and its controls, practical exercise and experience in driving results in a completely different type of knowing – an embodied knowing that does not require us to constantly think about what we are doing. To understand that knowing can be a type of doing and doing a type of knowing is essential for the understanding of listening. Listening is itself a type of doing and a type of knowing. The question is, what type? Driving a car or playing tennis can become a form of embodied knowing because they are themselves bodily activities. So are manual and artistic activities such as craftsmanship, playing a musical instrument, or painting. What we do with our bodies we can know how to do in a bodily way. But what sort of bodily activity is it that we engage in when we listen? We need to address this question to understand what sort of doing and what sort of knowing listening is or can be. Usually this question is side-tracked by arguing that listening is an activity of the 'whole person', of body and mind working in harmony. If this is so however, then what is the bodily side of this 'holistic' functioning? What is the bodily knowing that ensures that our listening is holistic and not just a purely mental activity of construing, interpreting and representing?

This is a difficult question to answer because listening confronts us not primarily as a form of doing, bodily or mental, but a form of *not-doing* – of keeping still physically, refraining from speech, and restraining also our inner speech and mental activity. Is listening then a 'psycho-physical' or emotional activity? Is it 'empathy'? If so, what sort of psycho-physical activity is this 'empathy'? A therapeutic listener can only 'empathically' sense a client's feelings by *feeling* them. We can only sense discomfort in another person because we ourselves feel discomforted by the other's discomfort. Our own discomfort is quite distinct from the discomfort that affects the other person, but it is not *separable* from it. Were our own feelings not merely distinct but entirely separate from other people's, there would be no possibility of 'empathy'. Given then that our bodily empathy or resonance with another person comes to us through an awareness of something that *we* feel, how do we respond to this feeling? We can repress, ignore or put the feeling to one side. As a result we are likely to express it indirectly – to 'act it out'. Or we can detach from our own feeling of discomfort and see it as something 'caused' by and therefore really belonging to the other person. We respond then by asking the other person how they feel, or helping them through therapeutic techniques or feedback to 'get in touch with their feelings'. But in this way we do not respond directly to the discomfort we feel. Again we express our own discomfort only indirectly – by getting the other person to express theirs. In neither case are we listening and responding to our own feeling of discomfort. To do so means neither repressing it in silence or getting others to express it verbally. It means responding to that feeling of discomfort in our bodies in a bodily way – bodying it. To listen and respond to our own bodily feelings – whatever or whoever we see them as triggered by – is to feel them. To feel them is to respond to them in a bodily way – to body them. But bodying a feeling means not only acknowledging it mentally but finding a way of being in our bodies that allows us to *be* them and in this sense contain them. The therapist's ability to be with others is dependent on their capacity to be a body, to feel with their bodies, and to respond to these bodily feelings in a bodily way so as to stay with them. By being with our feelings in a bodily way – by bodying them – they transform us and we transform them. We do not just 'have' feelings or 'attribute' hypothetical feelings to others. *We* feel, and are transformed by being with and bodying that feeling. It is this ability to be with and body a feeling that helps others to trust their feelings and feel safe in 'being in touch' with them.

Listening is not representational knowledge – knowing 'that' I or you feel something, or knowing 'about' my or your feelings. Nor, however, is it a type of pragmatic knowing based on doing – doing something with my mind or doing something with my body. Physical expression and mental repression of feelings are both forms of doing. Listening is a type of knowing based not on a physical or mental activity of doing but on our activity of *being*. Acts of being involve either identification, dis-identification, or staying in contact with feelings – being with them. *Being with* a feeling means 'knowing it' in an intimate bodily way – 'bodying' it. It results in a transformation of both our being and of the feeling itself – and it is this transformation that generates insights and comprehensions, that can be represented and expressed in words. Listening as 'being a body' and as 'bodying' allows us not only to really feel what we feel but to think it and speak it. Our bodies are in constant flux and change – responding continuously to our environment, to our minds and thoughts, and to other people. The ego wants to remain detached from this flux and yet seeks knowledge 'about' its environment and other people. It does not recognise that it is our own being that is constantly in flux – constantly becoming – that it is we who constantly *body* or *disembody* this becoming. The changing 'experience', 'feelings' and 'perceptions' that our 'bodyminds' give us are ours to either know in a bodily way or in a mental way – to body or to represent in a disembodied way as 'knowledge'. To paraphrase Heidegger, it is *we* that 'body' or 'disembody' who we are – not the 'mind' or 'the body'. It is not our bodies that cause our feelings or 'pick up' the feelings of others. It is *we* who choose to be or not be a body, to feel or not feel with our bodies – to know or not know in this bodily way.

In listening we intend to know each other's mind. We cannot 'read' each other's minds so we listen. But our bodies constantly read each other's bodies – and this helps us to know each other's minds in a way that is deeper than just mental knowing, knowing 'that'. The listener who 'knows' is a listener who knows his or her own feelings because he or she can be with them and body them.

We speak of someone giving us a 'knowing' look or glance. That is not because they read our minds, but because in this look they embody their body's own knowing in a bodily way. The listener who knows 'tacitly' how to listen is a listener whose listening is itself a type of silent knowing. This listener is a *knowing listener* – one who *chooses* to know in a bodily way and whose physical presence therefore silently embodies and communicates this knowing. The knowing listener does not know all there is to know 'about' other people's feelings. But nor does he or she pretend to be a black slate of unknowing, a 'disinterested' listener. The knowing listener knows that, whatever feelings are encountered in the encounter with the other, to be with and to body them is also to transform them and be transformed by them. Knowing listeners are *knowing* listeners because they know themselves as *transforming* listeners. Listening, I have argued, is non-representational anticipation of what is to be heard. What the therapeutic listener anticipates – pre-cognises – is a not another person's words or state of being but a transformation – a becoming. A transformation can only be anticipated because the therapeutic listener is a knowing listener – a person who allows themselves to *knowingly undergo a transformation* in the very process of listening. We become knowing and 'therapeutic' listeners not because we perceive, ask or talk about feelings, but because we have the courage to first of all body these feelings and let them transform our being. Our thoughts and emotions are transformed into *tones of being* which resonate with and touch the other in their essential being.

25. Hosting the Daemon
— the listening body and the listening self

Initially the baby experiences itself as part of a sonorous and tactile *field*. Inner sounds are experienced 'externally' and outer sounds experienced 'internally'. Both are experienced in a *tactile* way. A creaking tree branch, for example, is felt as a penetrating and electric touch, which excites from within. But what or who touches what or who? This 'inner vibrational touch' abolishes distance – it makes no difference that the tree is outside the window rubbing the pane of glass. Nor does the baby attach external verbal labels to these phenomena which help to locate them in space or time. 'Window' and 'tree' are words, but we are speaking of an infant (Latin *in-fans* : not-speaking).

Hearing through inner vibrational touch works 'inside out'. We first identify *with* the 'thing' and only secondly identify 'what' thing it is – if we have words to call it by. Before we know what to call it, however, it already calls us. The call touches us and resonates within us. Vibrations may come from music, voices or the awareness of cellular activity. For the foetus, the waters of the womb are such a fluid vibrational medium, a resonant field. In the womb this resonant field surrounds the 'listening body' of the foetus as its physical medium. After birth the infant's body becomes the womb of its self-experience – with a psychic interiority or somatic 'inner space' in which it experiences its own feeling tones. This is the *psyche-soma* in Winnicott's sense.

When the umbilical cord is cut at birth our connection with the physical womb of the mother is severed. Our being-in-the-womb becomes a being-in-the-world. This is mediated by our being-in-the-body, by the *psyche-soma*. As we begin to dwell within a world denoted and configured by language, however our 'being-in-the-world' becomes a 'being-in-the-word'. This process is set in train by the parent's listening, which becomes a verbal rather than a musical listening. At first the mother attunes to the infant's gurgles and babble as musical communications of feeling tones –

as voice music. The communication she engages in with the baby is a communication of feeling tone expressed through sound, through the mutual gaze, and through touch and handling. This is the intermediate area between 'direct' and 'indirect' communication that Winnicott spoke of – 'physiognomic communication'. Gradually however, the mother and other adults seek to interpret the infant's sounds not as expressions of a tonal communication but as words which call things name and call for things by their name. If verbal communication simply replaces or becomes opposed to what Winnicott called silent communication, it is in this process that mind and body, intellect and emotions, persona and psyche-soma can part company – that the rift between language and being can grow. When this happens the individual cannot experience language as a second body. Instead it becomes an alien skin or a verbal mask, a fashionable garment or ideological uniform, a manipulative tool or object.

Our understanding of a word is not itself a word nor is it a thing – an object. And yet for the intellect the meaning of the word becomes some *thing* that is named by other *words*. This mutually signifying network of signifiers becomes a self-sufficient entity – the 'language mind'- breaking the link between intellect and psyche-soma. Only inward listening can re-link and unite the psychic interiority of the bodily experience (inner sensation and feeling tone) and the inner dimensions of meaning that open up within language. To experience the word as a second body is no longer to experience language and mind as something purely 'mental' – a two-dimensional nexus of signifiers – but as the three dimensional surface of a body of meaning. This 'body of meaning' unites the inner meaning space of language and mind (the 'mental body') with the meaningful psychic interiority of the physical body (the 'psychic body'), creating a single 'body of meaning'.

The key to experiencing the word as a second body is appreciation that the body of a word is its sounds. The meaning of words as sounds which unites and transcends their meanings as words – unites and transcends verbal opposites. The word field of the 'm' sound, for example, like that of any speech sound, included groups of *words* with opposing senses: *malignant, glum, morbid, morose* vs. *remedy, warmth, womb, comfort,* Sounds unite what words divide. That is why mystical tradition has always recognised a hidden meaning and healing potency to speech sounds. This is to do with the way in which their metaphysical connotations transcend verbal and emotional dichotomies and polarities. It is the basis of the belief in 'words of power' or 'mantra'.

The sounds that the baby produces are not words but shapes or *bodies* of feeling tone. Through them it learns to per-sonify its own feeling tones (*per-sona* – through sound). It also learns to embody these feeling tones. For it is through tactile and proprioceptive exploration of the oral cavity that the baby begins to distinguish between its *own* bodily sounds and those of the objects and people surrounding it. By embodying feeling tones as sounds they gain a sense of their own physical boundaries. This is how feelings come to be experienced as dimension of being contained and experienced somatically. The oral cavity is truly the 'mouth of creation', for it is the means by which tactile feeling (verb) becomes feelings (noun).

What is called 'mystical' philosophy attempts to preserve an understanding of the meaningfulness of elementary sounds and of the meaning of health as 'soundness' (*Gesundheit*). The words *mute, mystery, mysticism* and *mystical* are rooted in the Greek syllable 'mu', a syllable which also names the letter of the alphabet signifying the 'm' sound. The 'm' sound is one we make with the mouth closed. The Greek word for 'initiates' is *mustai* – 'the close-mouthed ones'. It refers to those who bear the secrets of the mysteries in silence, their lips sealed.

Those who listen may appear mute. That does not mean they do not listen or do not speak to us through their listening. For we do not need to open our mouths or make any sounds aloud in order to use sound to compose ourselves when we listen and to psychically tone and tune our listening. The sounds of our listening are not actual sounds but virtual sounds – the tones that would and do resound when our breath (psyche) produces listening noises such as 'hmm' and 'hnn'. The Greek syllable 'mu' was also a word. It denoted an audible exhalation – 'groan' or 'sigh'. The 'hums' and 'hahs' of the listener are not simply 'phatic communication' – ways of signalling to the speaker that we are paying attention. They are a sort of virtual speech. The tone of our audible hums and groans outwardly echo and communicate the inner tone of our being as we listen – the tone of our listening. In modulating the tone of our 'hums' and 'hahs' we also indirectly modulate the tone of our listening.

Heidegger spoke of the 'unified realm of essence' connoted by the many Greek words containing the 'life-root' *za* (e.g. *zatheos* – 'hallowed'). He was aware that if we listen carefully to the sounds of which words are composed, we can hear in them connotations linking them with the entire field of other words containing those same sounds. And yet sounds do not 'have' meanings in the same way that words do. Like dream images they *gather* and *condense* meanings which words and verbal denotations divide and polarise. It is only by listening to a whole 'sym-phony' of words containing a common sound that we can sense the metaphysical essence of this sound. The symphony of 'm' for example includes: *permeation, amnion, womb, warmth, mellow, memory, medium, meditation, meaning, mother, mantra.* This is why the connotations of a particular sound cannot be defined in words – only heard and responded to. For any word we might choose to define the phonaesthetic value of a particular sound (for example 'mellow' to define the 'm') would impose connotations belonging to its other sounds (the 'l' sound for example).

This word-field of a sound breaks up into 'sense-groups' – sub-groups of words each of which express a common dimension of meaning. In the case of the 'b' sound for example we have on the one hand *boundary, barrier, border, membrane, bubble, balloon* and on the other hand *burst, break, blurt, dribble, embarrass.* The words which make up such sense groups may or may not be etymologically related. From them we can nevertheless discern a 'root sense' or metaphysical essence. With the 'b' sound, for example, we can see a common thread running through all the sense groups. This has to do with different possible relationships to boundaries and boundedness – staying within them (*abiding,*

163

being), challenging them (*barrage, battle*), overstepping them (*blush, embarrass*).

In one sense this is surprising. After all, in making the 'b' sound we both create a boundary – by sealing our lips – and then allow this b̲arrier to b̲urst. It is as if the different sense groups themselves express the different meanings with which this bodily sound can be imbued – a b̲ellowing 'b' versus a b̲ashful 'b' for example. Bodily sounds, in other words, are themselves meaningful – we can do and say things with them that are expressed in the words that contain them. It is as if the words contain a given sound are metaphors of the meanings we can enact and embody in making that sound. That is not to say that everytime we use a word containing an 'b' sound we are dribbling or blowing bubbles. The *manner* in which we make a 'b' sound can constitute not only a physical act such blowing or dribbling, or a vocal act like bellowing or booming, but also a social acts such as boasting or bragging or an 'inward' acts such as brooding. The physical act of making a particular sound is itself a metaphorical communication. And although we do not speak by uttering individual phonemes but by combining these in words, words are also metaphors of the meaning potentials of their own sounds – the meanings these sounds can *embody* through the manner in which they are uttered.

Meditational and healing practices have in various ways combined or emphasised the role of silent *intent* on the one hand and audible or embodied *expression* (mantra, music, chant and gesture) on the other. The word *mantra* has two roots: *man* – to be aware, and *trana* – liberation from bondage. The Sanskrit *man* is the root syllable of all those Indo-European words connected with *mind* and the root of the word *man* itself. (Sanskrit *manus* – individual). It is also embodied in the Sanskrit *manas* – sense or meaning. In fact *man, mind, and meaning* are all essentially linked by a common yet intangible thread of 'meaning' mysteriously embodied in the 'm' and 'n' sounds themselves. The meaning of a *mantram* does not lie in its verbal definition, but in the way it calls us to thought and calls us to listen in a way which transcends definitions. By exploring its *logos* – the meanings it gathers and condenses through its sounds and their word fields – we experience an inward expansion of the meaning within the word. Etymology gives us clues and hints in this exploration, but only if we are able to receive this hint – to listen.

Heidegger was accused by his critics of being the philosopher of the *single word*. This is easy to understand, since for him words like 'being', and 'language' were not technical or academic terms reducible to a finite and formulaic meaning. Instead they were indeed *mantra*. Meditations on a particular keywords or mantra allowed him to bring to light hidden *inner* relationships between this word and others. These inner connections were suggested by etymological links, for it is these which are the 'wormholes' of the word, linking different dimensions of meaning in the body of the word – its sound and root syllables. Heidegger did not chant his mantra or define them etymologically – he listened to them and to their etymological resonances, tuning himself poetically to their 'inner sound'.

Thinking as *poiesis* is an oscillation between words and wordlessness. This oscillation has its own 'inner sound' – the inner sound of our intent. Like the pre-verbal sounds of the baby, the inner sounds of our intent not only precede and anticipate verbal expression but also shape and colour our feeling tones – our psyche-somatic experience. That is the half-truth of 'positive thinking'. For in the use of hypnotic suggestion or verbal 'affirmations' to alter our mood, confidence and physical state it is not the mental words we use in speaking to ourselves that are effective so much as the intent behind those words.

The desire and intent behind our words can never be fully expressed in words. This is because of the way in which words polarise meaning. Thinking as thinking is not 'negative' or 'positive' – it is a way of listening that takes our comprehension of ourselves beyond such verbal opposites. This is a goal shared by many 'mysticisms'. It is also a way of being hinted at by the ordinary understanding of what it means to respond to life 'philosophically'. This does not imply resignation and acceptance as opposed to optimism or struggle. To *be* 'philosophical' is not the same thing as to be melancholic, dour or depressed, adopt a superficial positivity and cheerfulness or fired with manic enthusiasm. It does not mean posing unanswerable questions, finding unquestionable answers or engaging in endless intellectual debate. For none of these poles involves the type of questing, and thoughtful inward listening that belong to the essence of philosophy.

Mental and physical ill-health cannot be 'cured' by magically chanting mantras, striking a few gongs or meditating on the sound of a tuning fork. And yet health is essentially soundness (*Ge-sund-heit*). This soundness has to do with our inward listening – the relation between the 'inner sound' of our intent and the mental or spoken words with which we verbalise this intent. Both affect our tone of being, psychically and somatically. Both confused thinking and thinking dominated by superficial verbal constructs and opposites will muddy or distort our feeling tones and thereby affect our body tone – whether in a generalised or localised way. Bad health is bad music – bad mind music and bad body music. Conversely, however, music that may first seem to us to be quite un-musical and un-healthy can conceal a rich and meaningful musical intelligence and purpose. Healing in this case does not necessarily mean 'changing our tune', swopping one type of physical or mental music for another more 'positive' or 'healthy' sort. It means learning to hear, appreciate and affirm the sort of music that we *are*.

People come to doctors, psychiatrist, analysts and counsellors, not essentially for pills or even for words but with a need to be heard. They seek in the professional helper either an embodiment of their own listening self – or a way of continuing to overhear their own listening body. What I call **hearkening** and **heeding, holding** and **handling, with-holding and hinting** are ways of hallowing our minds and bodies and making them whole by deepening our listening. To heal is to become is to whole, to overcome rifts in our being. We cannot do this without understanding and undermining ourselves the rift between language and being that characterises our society. This means finding a new listening relationship to language and to being. The result is that we liberate our listening body from the language mind and the language ego – from the speaking self. This is a long process, one through which ultimately both mind and body become **host** to a new self – the listening self.

The listening self is not Being, nor is it another human being. And yet it is our link with Being – and it *is* also a̲ being. It is not a part of us. We are a part of it. It is not an 'I', voice or sub-personality. Nor is it an object, even a 'self-object'. It is a you to which we are intimately related – a you that says 'we', and together with which we are a 'we'. When we hear ourselves speak we hear our own speaking self echoed. This may be a comfortable or uncomfortable experience. When we hear ourselves listen, we begin to sense the unplumbed depths of our own listening. The inward expansion of meaning that then unfolds – the inward expansion of our listening bodies – creates a womb. In this womb we can then become host to our listening self. The word 'host' is related to the Latin *hostis* – a stranger – it is from this that we get the word 'hostile'. To be a host to someone is to treat them with courtesy and respect. Listening is also a way of **hosting** someone. When we **hearken** to someone's presence and **heed** their words we prepare ourselves to become host to new aspects of our own being. The *hostility* to mysticism is a fear of **hosting** another self, a self that is not the speaking self and that is 'strange' to the language mind and the language ego. This is the 'self as another.' A *daemon* with no name – except perhaps *mu* .

One meaning of the verb 'to be' is 'to dwell'. A guest may be temporary or permanent. In counselling we offer a temporary dwelling to the listening self. Mystical philosophy seeks to give a more permanent abode to the being that dwells in our listening. This is not 'regression'. It does not mean 'returning to the womb' but becoming one – hosting the *daemon*.

Summary (A) — Languages of Being

1) Each of us not only has or speaks a language. Each of us *is* a language. The language that we *are* is our unique way of being – our 'language of being'.

2) Every individual 'language of being' like every verbal language or artistic medium offers infinite possibilities for expression. Our 'language of being' is our own unique but infinite potential for being.

3) Each of us translates our 'language of being' into languages that we acquire socially and then 'have' i.e. into the languages of verbal and physical behaviour (speech, voice, body language, social, professional and sexual behaviour etc.)

4) A translation can be more or less true to the original. So too can our own behaviour, our words and actions, be more or less an authentic expression of our essential way of being – our 'language of being'.

5) Every verbal language shares common meanings with others. Each individual's essential language of being shares common *values* with that of others. Essential values belong to our 'language of being' – they can never be reduced to words or defined by moral laws or codes. They are shared potentials for being.

6) Values are like genes. Two or more people may share common genes even though they are not related biologically. Similarly, two or more people may share certain essential values, even though they are not related socially or speak different cultural, ideological, religious or professional languages.

7) Every verbal language colours and illuminates the meanings it expresses in a different way. That is why learning different languages (verbal, sensual and artistic) enriches us. Similarly each person's outward behaviour offers us a new 'vocabulary' for understanding and expressing ourselves. Understanding another human being means understanding their 'language'.

8) Authentic dialogue is always a double process of creative translation: (a) translating our own language of being into someone's else's words and behavioural language – experiencing our own being in their terms. (b) translating their values and way of being into our words and actions (experiencing their being in our terms). This translation process is creative – it helps both parties express and embody their own being in new ways.

9) A relationship is formed when two or more people share certain values, even though they express and embody these values in different ways and with different words and behaviours. Values are like the shared electrons that orbit both atoms in a molecular bond, and create a common electro-magnetic field.
10) Unlike each partner in a human bond both *donate* particular values to the shared 'bipersonal field' and *receive* certain values from it. The chemistry that connects people has to do not only with the values and potentials for being they already express and embody but with those they don't. The latter are like electron 'holes'. They are 'negative' values – unfulfilled potentials for being.

11) Another person cannot be a substitute for our own value fulfilment. They can contribute to that fulfilment only if we are capable of learning their language and speaking it. This means

receiving each other's essential values and letting them become part of our own being.

12) A relationship with another individual or a group can only be fulfilled outside the pair or group. A language student needs to practice with other people besides his or her teacher (pair relationship) or class (group). Similarly, individuals in a relationship only fully embody what they get from another person or persons *outside* that relationship or that group – alone or in other relationships and other groups.

13) Relationships break down because people resist receiving what another person or a group is giving them – do not embody it outside the relationship. Alternatively they may fail because one or other partner is unable to express and embody what they are giving to the other(s) – the values they are donating to the pair or group – in an acceptable way.

14) Meaning is rooted in being. People mean something to one another not because of psychological processes (e.g. 'projection' or 'transference') but because they *are* something for one another – they share common values or they express and embody each other's unrecognised and unfulfilled values.

15) 'Personality' is the way we express our language of being and 'bear forth' our values in words and deeds. 'Character' is our inner bearing – the values we bear within us and communicate wordlessly. Personality is the expression of our acquired languages. Character is the embodiment of our essential language of being.

16) Expression is distinct from embodiment. A person may be able to express a meaning like 'trust' or 'anger' but unable to contain and embody it as a value – to communicate it with their whole

being. Conversely, an individual may be able to wordlessly embody and silently communicate a value but unable to express it outwardly as a meaning in ordinary words or body language. Expression without embodiment is ungrounded and inauthentic. Embodiment without expression is mute or autistic.

17) Any given individual may show us ways of expressing and 'bearing forth' certain values that we ourselves can only embody and communicate silently. Or they may show us ways of embodying certain values that we can only 'act out' or talk *about*. Conversely, what we *mean* to other individuals is always linked with the values we express or embody for them.

18) For life to have meaning means allowing ourselves to *mean* and *be meant*.
We can say or do things without *meaning* them – without intending them as fulfilments of our being and its potentials. As a result they have no meaning or value for us. Conversely, things can happen to us or be done to us without us allowing ourselves to *be meant*. This implies being prepared to see meaning and value in them – to find a way of expressing this meaning and embodying this value.

19) The meaning, value and purpose of being is simply to be. The meaning of 'meaning' (noun) has to do with meaning (verb) – with intending or orienting our being towards something or someone beyond it. Every being quests not itself but the being of other beings. In this way it finds value in its own being.
20) To be 'oneself' means more than being 'one' self. It means relating to others and through them discovering one's own 'other selves'. The unity of a language is the inseparability of its words and the meanings they express, which form an interconnected

whole. The unity of our individuality is the in-dividuality and in-divisibility of these different selves – and the values they embody.

22) When we speak we combine words and letters belonging to the same language. Our 'language of being' is the inner alphabet and grammar of our physical existence, the different values or potentials of our being and their inter-connection. This is experienced through our dreams and through our pre-verbal awareness of objects, people and events.

23) There is an inner order of events which is not determined by cause and effect, by our childhood past, or by our genes. The sequence of notes, chords and instruments in a symphony is not shaped by cause and effect but by the aesthetic structure of the whole. Nor is the music just physical sound vibrations. The symphony is a sym-phony – a simultaneous gestalt of meaning which expresses the composer's language of being. Only by perceiving our lives in time aesthetically, as symphonic and synchronous wholes or 'gestalts' do we begin to appreciate our own language of being.

24) What shapes a symphony is the composer's intent and inner listening. What shapes the symphony of our lives is our inner intent and inner hearing – the way we hear ourselves, compose ourselves and then play our own music. Our bodies are the instrument through which we both hear and play the feeling tones of this music – they embody this music and can thus express it.

25) What words and notes divide, our listening unites. What different languages, cultures and sciences divide, our listening can unite. Listening links us inwardly to a language before language – the primal language or 'aesthetic' of our being.

Summary (B) — Listening and Being

(1)

Listening cannot be reduced to a set of skills, techniques or abilities. To do so implies that for the speaker it makes no essential difference *who* the listener *is* – that the only important thing is *how* and how 'well' they listen. This is a fundamental and false separation of listening and *being*.

(2)

Listening is not just 'attending' to someone but also intending them – meaning this person and no other as the focus of my listening. To listen is to 'list' or lean with one's whole being towards another. This is not a question of 'body language'. The bodily character of our listening reflects our inner bearing – the way we bear ourselves in silence, and lean inwardly towards each other in that silence. Our inner bearing as listeners is the basis of both our intellectual and emotional positions and our physical postures. It sets the *tone* of our listening.

(3)

*To listen with our whole being means to communicate our whole being — the essence of who we **are**.* In tuning our whole being to another, therefore, we not only harmonise with the tone of the speaker (outer rapport) – we also communicate the essential tone of our own being. Inner rapport arises from an interplay and harmony of the contrasting tones of being conveyed by speaker and listener. As listeners we silently 'sound out' each other with our own essential tone. Tones of being are the inner wavelengths of attunement on which all communication, verbal and non-verbal, rides. They are the basic carrier waves on which messages are both received and *transmitted* by the listener.

> *"From tones at variance comes perfect harmony."*
> Heraclitus

(4)

Listening is not just 'following' others as they speak. We cannot follow others unless we stay with ourselves as we follow – remain inwardly attuned to our own being and its inner voice. By staying in touch with ourselves as we listen we *lead* as well as follow with our listening, for in this way we encourage the speaker to stay in touch with their own being as they speak – to be led by their own inner voice rather than losing themselves in words.

(5)

Listening does not simply precede and prepare our outward response to others. It is a form of direct inner response – a communication of being. The way we perceive someone as we listen communicates through the inner bearing and inner tones of our listening. It is this that is embodied in our physical posture and voice tone.

(6)

Listening is not just saying nothing; not-speaking. It is an active form of 'un-saying'- of leaving things unsaid. What is unsaid is also 'un-said' – left for the speaker to 'pick up'. By restraining immediate verbal response we withhold only the intellectual and emotional *translation* of our inner response. If we are really in contact with another person, this inner response will communicate wordlessly – by modulating the tone of being we convey as listeners.

(7)

Listening is not something we do in between stretches of speaking. It is what we do in order to heed words *after* they have been spoken, and to hear our own unspoken thoughts and feelings *before* we voice them.

> *"Although this inner word is ever-present, men fail to comprehend it, both before hearing it and after they have heard."*

> Heraclitus

(8)

To listen is not just to 'hear someone out' – to not interrupt or foreclose their speech. It is to grant time to listen to what their words are saying – to let *them* speak to us. This requires an interval of silence *after* the other has finished speaking and *before* we respond in words. Without intervals of silence we do not allow time for our response to form – for inner impressions to gather and questions to gestate. Withholding immediate response allows us to *hearken* to another human being and to really *heed* their words.

"Not knowing how to listen, neither can they speak."
Heraclitus

(9)

Listening means neither judging nor remaining neutral towards someone's words. It means being sensitive to the ever-present gap between language and being. To be 'understanding' towards someone's words means to stand under them – to hear them as translations of their own being and therefore open to questioning. Many ways of speaking about ourselves are poor translations – they are substitutes for listening. And when words fail us we look for different words – new labels and categories – instead of attending to our own wordless knowing. Different registers of language may then substitute for different ways of listening.

(10)

Listening cannot be replaced by answering someone's questions, echoing these questions or posing our own questions to them, however 'open'. Listening is not verbal questioning or answering but the wordless *questing* of our being as it seeks expression in language. It is not people but language itself – the habitual words we use to formulate our questions and answers – that listening silently questions. Ask a verbal question and the answer will reflect the terms of that question. Ask a silent question and we can hear a silent answer – hear another person's words as a translation of their language of being.

(11)

Listening is not a counselling or therapeutic role. To listen fully means to listen with our whole being. This is more than just listening 'in role' – listening *as* a counsellor, *as* a teacher, *as* a manager etc. As long as we are merely listening 'as' we are not really listening *to* someone or *with* them. What we listen *for* – what we *quest* in our listening – is instead determined by our role.

(12)

Listening with our whole being means listening with our bodies and not just our minds. The speaking self listens with the mind, framing meanings in its own mental terms or echoing the words of others. The listening self attends both to sounds and to silence with the body – really hearing what has been said. Listening with the body means being able to fully bear and embody ourselves in silence – to find an inner bearing in which we can *be* in silence and hearken to others within it.

(13)

Listening is not 'hearing' or 'understanding'. We listen when we do not hear or do not fully understand. As soon as we think we have heard or understood it is easy to stop listening. To *hearken* means to maintain a centre of absolute stillness and silence within ourselves – a continuous sense of *not* fully hearing or understanding. It is from this still point that we connect with others through 'silver threads of silence' – the tendrils of our listening body.

(14)

Listening does not require giving 'body signals' to the speaker. Only by *holding* to a particular physical posture do we really become body aware – able to fully feel this bodily posture and distinguish it from our inner bearing. The less bodily movements we make the more mobile this inner bearing becomes. Holding is not 'rigidity' – it frees the inner mobility and motility of our listening body.

Other Books and Articles by Peter Wilberg

Heidegger, Medicine and 'Scientific Method'
New Gnosis Publications 2005

The Therapist as Listener – Heidegger and the Missing Dimension of Counselling and Psychotherapy Training
New Gnosis Publications 2005

Heidegger, Phenomenology and Indian Thought
New Gnosis Publications 2008

The Illness is the Cure - an introduction to Life Medicine & Life Doctoring - a new existential approach to illness
New Yoga Publications 2013

Meditation and Mental Health – an introduction to Awareness Based Cognitive Therapy
New Yoga Publications 2010

from PSYCHOSOMATICS to SOMA-SEMIOTICS - Felt Sense and the Sensed Body in Medicine and Psychotherapy New Yoga Publications 2010

The Awareness Principle – a Radical New Philosophy of Life, Science and Religion New Yoga Publications 2008

The QUALIA Revolution – from Quantum Physics to Qualia Science Second Edition, New Gnosis Publications 2008

Tantra Reborn – The Sensuality and Sexuality of our Immortal Soul Body New Yoga Publications 2009

The New Yoga of Awareness – Tantric Wisdom for Today's World
New Yoga Publications 2209

The Science Delusion – Why God is Real and Science is Religious Myth New Gnosis Publications 2008

Event Horizon – Terror, Tantra and the Ultimate Metaphysics of Awareness New Yoga Publications 2008

Deep Socialism – A New Manifesto of Marxist Ethics and Economics New Gnosis Publications 2003

From New Age to New Gnosis – Towards a New Gnostic Spirituality New Gnosis Publications 2003

Head, Heart and Hara – the Soul Centres of West and East New Gnosis Publications, 2003

Articles:

The Language of Listening
Journal of the Society for Existential Analysis 3

Introduction to Maieutic Listening
Journal of the Society for Existential Analysis 8.1

Listening as Bodywork
Energy and Character; Journal of Biosynthesis 30/2

The Language of Listening
Journal of the Society for Existential Analysis 3

From Existential Psychotherapy to Existential Medicine Journal of the Society for Existential Analysis 22.2

See also **www.heidegger.org.uk**

www.existentialmedicine.org

Made in the USA
Coppell, TX
28 February 2024

29567019R00105